Continuous Integration and Delivery with Test-driven Development

Cultivating quality, speed, and collaboration through automated pipelines

Amit Bhanushali

Alekhya Achanta

Beena Bhanushali

www.bpbonline.com

FIRST EDITION 2024

ISBN: 978-93-5551-972-6

Distributors:

BPB PUBLICATIONS
20, Ansari Road, Darya Ganj
New Delhi-110002
Ph: 23254990/23254991

DECCAN AGENCIES
4-3-329, Bank Street,
Hyderabad-500195
Ph: 24756967/24756400

MICRO MEDIA
Shop No. 5, Mahendra Chambers,
150 DN Rd. Next to Capital Cinema,
V.T. (C.S.T.) Station, MUMBAI-400 001
Ph: 22078296/22078297

Published by Manish Jain for BPB Publications, 20 Ansari Road, Darya Ganj, New Delhi-110002 and Printed by him at Manipal Technologies, Manipal

www.bpbonline.com

Dedicated to

Our loving parents and teachers who taught us the basics of life and science

About the Authors

- **Amit Bhanushali**, a seasoned Quality Assurance Manager with 22 years of expertise, has excelled in Software Quality Optimization, particularly in the BFSI and higher education sectors. His proficiency spans automation testing, performance testing, and navigating complex DevOps and CI/CD environments, integrating cutting-edge technologies like AI and ML. With a Master's degree in Business Data Analytics from West Virginia University, Amit seamlessly combines academic insights with practical acumen. His impactful collaborations with Fortune 500 companies showcase a transformative blend of theoretical knowledge and hands-on experience. As a leader at West Virginia University, he has successfully spearheaded projects, reducing costs and enhancing education quality. Beyond his managerial role, Amit has authored research papers and novels on Software Quality Optimization, Automation Testing, AI, and ML. Recognized with the Innovator of the Year award at the Globee Business Awards 2023, his journey epitomizes innovation, leadership, and enduring transformation, making him a deserving recipient of the International Achiever Award.

- **Alekhya Achanta** is a Senior DataOps Engineer with expertise in BI, visualization, and data-driven decision-making. She creates robust data pipelines, dashboards, and actionable insights that optimize business outcomes. She is proficient in Python, SQL, data visualization, and tools like Matillion, DBT, and Power BI. She has an MS in Data Science, published 10+ scholarly papers in leading international journals, and recognized as a Top Voice on LinkedIn in Data Science. She received numerous accolades for the companies she worked with across the years for her intellectual curiosity and passion for problem-solving. With her strong technical expertise coupled with an ability to understand business needs, she delivers cutting-edge data solutions that create real impact. Alekhya mentors ADPList and is a proud IEEE Senior Member.

- **Beena Bhanushali** is a highly skilled Salesforce CRM Administrator with a focus on optimizing Salesforce implementations for business growth. Specializing in CI/CD methodologies within the Salesforce ecosystem, Beena excels in streamlining processes and enhancing user experiences. With a keen eye for detail and problem-solving abilities, she collaborates effectively with cross-functional teams to deliver scalable solutions that meet clients' unique needs. Known for her commitment to staying abreast of industry trends, Beena is recognized as a trusted expert in Salesforce, making her an invaluable asset to any project or team.

About the Reviewers

- **Shantanu Neema** is an accomplished data scientist, recognized for delivering impactful insights in diverse industries through data-driven methodologies. With a proficiency in managing and analyzing datasets to define precise business use cases, he excels in crafting solutions for intricate challenges spanning real estate, energy, transportation, environmental compliance, and manufacturing. Shantanu's extensive experience encompasses the entire data science process, culminating in model deployment using cloud infrastructure. His expertise extends to a robust foundation in CI/CD, ML pipelines, and testing methodologies, ensuring the efficiency and resilience of his solutions. Beyond his technical role, Shantanu actively engages as a researcher and serves as a technical reviewer for books centered around CI/CD, data science, and Python. This commitment underscores his dedication to advancing best practices and fostering innovation in these dynamic fields. Shantanu Neema invites readers to explore his insights and contributions, encapsulated within the pages of publications that reflect his ongoing pursuit of excellence in data science and technology.

- **Dr. Nalini Jagtap** is a distinguished academician with over 8 years of teaching experience, serving as an Associate Professor at Dr D Y Patil Institute of Engineering Management and Research. She holds a Doctorate in Computer Engineering from Savitribai Phule Pune University, where she was ranked first in her Master's program. Her dedication to academic excellence is truly commendable.

  Dr. Nalini Jagtap's impressive background in academia is underscored by remarkable achievements in research and teaching. With expertise spanning Computer Vision and Pattern Recognition, as well as Artificial Intelligence and Machine Learning, Dr. Jagtap has established herself as a leading figure in these fields. Demonstrating exceptional teaching prowess throughout her 8 years of experience, Dr. Jagtap has imparted knowledge across various subjects.

In addition to her academic endeavors, Dr. Jagtap has made substantial contributions to the IT industry, showcasing her versatility and adaptability over 7.5 years in various roles. She combines academic excellence with extensive practical experience. Beyond her academic and professional accomplishments, Dr. Jagtap has significantly contributed to the advancement of her field through influential research papers, a testament to her deep-rooted background in research.

Acknowledgement

We are grateful to BPB Publications for their guidance and expertise in bringing this book to fruition. Revising this book was a long journey, with valuable participation and collaboration of reviewers, technical experts, and editors.

We would also like to acknowledge the valuable contributions of our mentors and colleagues during many years working in the tech industry, who have taught us so much and provided valuable feedback on our work.

Special gratitude is extended to Dr. Nalini Jagtap and Shantanu Neema for their invaluable contributions as technical reviewers. Dr. Nalini Jagtap, with over 8 years of teaching experience and a Doctorate in Computer Engineering, provided insightful feedback reflecting her dedication to academic excellence, particularly in computer vision and AI. Meanwhile, Shantanu Neema, an accomplished Data Scientist, demonstrated his expertise in managing and analyzing datasets across diverse industries, including real estate, energy, transportation, environmental compliance, and manufacturing. His proficiency in model deployment on cloud infrastructure and implementation of CI/CD, ML pipelines, and testing methodologies greatly enhanced the quality of the work. Their combined efforts significantly enriched the research and academic endeavors.

Finally, we would like to thank all the readers who have taken an interest in our book and for their support in making it a reality. Your encouragement has been invaluable.

Preface

The landscape of software development has transformed radically, with customer expectations for faster delivery of high-quality digital products intensifying exponentially. Much as strict protocols govern safety-critical systems, today's complex web and mobile ecosystems demand stringent quality practices underpinned by comprehensive testing. Yet many resources focus excessively on theory without addressing practical application.

This hands-on guide bridges that gap, offering practitioners an invaluable inside understanding of how leading organizations optimize software and data CI/CD pipelines to accelerate release cycles without compromising stability or user experience. Balancing cutting-edge technical foundations with indispensable cultural transformation, the book equips enterprises to actualize the DevOps mandate of fail-fast innovation, seamless collaboration, and ruthless automation.

With continuous practices now an indispensable pillar of IT strategy, these pages detail battle-tested frameworks for quality engineering tailored to modern release trains. Through expert coverage of must-have toolchains as well as processes that safeguard both velocity and verification, readers will grasp not only CI/CD's immense potential but also its practical implementation and governance.

Complimenting conceptual mastery with actionable playbooks, this book illuminates the synergy between lean culture, behavioral best practices, and optimized pipelines. Readers will gain unprecedented clarity into the real-world changes necessary to retool release processes, test automation, and team dynamics that many Continuous Delivery initiatives overlook to their detriment.

Whether a novice seeking fundamental fluency or a leader charging towards DevOps excellence, this guide delivers the definitive reference for unlocking CI/CD's total value. The future of software lies in empathy, quality, and flow; it is our privilege to light the path forward.

Chapter 1: Adopting a Test-driven Development Mindset – Testing is an integral part of the **software development lifecycle (SDLC)**. As IT professionals, adopting a test-driven mindset enables us to deliver higher quality software through rapid feedback loops. In this chapter, we introduce the readers to **test-driven development (TDD)** methodology and contrast it with traditional testing approaches. Furthermore, we delve into the significance of data in modern software development and introduce the concept of DataOps, which emphasizes the importance of data operations in the agile development process.

Chapter 2: Understanding CI/CD Concepts – This chapter discusses the fundamental concepts of **continuous integration and continuous delivery (CI/CD)**, as well as the emerging paradigm of data CI/CD. Exploring the principles and benefits of CI/CD and data CI/CD, readers will gain a comprehensive understanding of how these practices streamline software and data workflows. They will learn how CI/CD practices enhance software quality while data CI/CD focuses on ensuring data integrity, quality, and reliability. By the end of this chapter, readers will be prepared to embrace both CI/CD and data CI/CD as integral components of modern software and data development, fostering efficiency, collaboration, and quality.

Chapter 3: Building the CI/CD Pipeline – This chapter discusses the intricacies of CI, CD, and data CI/CD, emphasizing their pivotal role in contemporary software development. We will guide you through the meticulous process of crafting a resilient CI/CD pipeline that integrates code and ensures seamless delivery of data. From the initial stages of code writing and testing to the final product delivery, we illuminate the critical elements that bolster code quality, uniformity, and swift deployment. By harnessing the power of this comprehensive system, development teams can significantly reduce manual interventions, leading to minimized errors and expedited results. With the added dimension of data CI/CD, we ensure that applications are always fueled by the most current and accurate data, enhancing overall productivity.

Chapter 4: Ensuring Effective CD – In this chapter, we cover the critical aspects of CD, focusing on both software and data. We explore topics related to real-time monitoring, observability practices, robust security measures, and strategic release management. By mastering the content of this chapter, readers will be well-equipped to navigate the complexities of modern CD, ensuring not only the seamless deployment of software but also safeguarding its integrity, optimizing performance, and ensuring compliance with industry standards.

Chapter 5: Optimizing CI/CD Practices – From addressing the unique demands of expansive projects and diverse environments to fostering an unyielding commitment to continuous improvement, this chapter equips readers to elevate their CI/CD endeavors. By absorbing the insights and strategies offered within these pages, readers are primed to optimize their CI/CD practices for both software and data, ensuring smoother delivery and consistent refinement of processes and outcomes.

Chapter 6: Specialized CI/CD Applications – From delving into mobile and IoT contexts to leveraging an arsenal of tools and embracing best practices, this chapter equips readers to navigate the terrain of specialized CI/CD domains. Armed with the insights garnered from this chapter, readers will be poised to implement CI/CD solutions tailored to distinct contexts, fostering efficiency, innovation, and excellence.

Chapter 7: Model Operations: DevOps Pipeline Case Studies – This chapter presents a collection of case studies that shed light on real-world applications of CI/CD practices. By examining these cases, readers will glean insights into how various organizations and projects have harnessed CI/CD to achieve remarkable outcomes, fostering innovation, reliability, and accelerated delivery.

Chapter 8: Data CI/CD: Emerging Trends and Roles – In closing, while the technical disciplines of CI/CD are essential, it is also vital that organizations nurture a collaborative culture focused on software quality, speed, and responsiveness to customer needs. Technical professionals should advocate for and model these values. By combining automated pipelines with cultural transformation, IT organizations can unlock the full benefits of CI/CD.

Code Bundle and Coloured Images

Please follow the link to download the
Code Bundle and the *Coloured Images* of the book:

https://rebrand.ly/hm0s5m1

The code bundle for the book is also hosted on GitHub at **https://github.com/bpbpublications/Continuous-Integration-and-Delivery-with-Test-driven-Development** In case there's an update to the code, it will be updated on the existing GitHub repository.

We have code bundles from our rich catalogue of books and videos available at **https://github.com/bpbpublications**. Check them out!

Errata

We take immense pride in our work at BPB Publications and follow best practices to ensure the accuracy of our content to provide with an indulging reading experience to our subscribers. Our readers are our mirrors, and we use their inputs to reflect and improve upon human errors, if any, that may have occurred during the publishing processes involved. To let us maintain the quality and help us reach out to any readers who might be having difficulties due to any unforeseen errors, please write to us at :

errata@bpbonline.com

Your support, suggestions and feedbacks are highly appreciated by the BPB Publications' Family.

Piracy

If you come across any illegal copies of our works in any form on the internet, we would be grateful if you would provide us with the location address or website name. Please contact us at **business@bpbonline.com** with a link to the material.

If you are interested in becoming an author

If there is a topic that you have expertise in, and you are interested in either writing or contributing to a book, please visit **www.bpbonline.com**. We have worked with thousands of developers and tech professionals, just like you, to help them share their insights with the global tech community. You can make a general application, apply for a specific hot topic that we are recruiting an author for, or submit your own idea.

Reviews

Please leave a review. Once you have read and used this book, why not leave a review on the site that you purchased it from? Potential readers can then see and use your unbiased opinion to make purchase decisions. We at BPB can understand what you think about our products, and our authors can see your feedback on their book. Thank you!

For more information about BPB, please visit **www.bpbonline.com**.

Table of Contents

CHAPTER 1

Adopting a Test-driven Development Mindset

Introduction

The purpose of this chapter is to define different approaches to software testing and to outline the pros and cons of each approach. Software development and testing are integral and closely related aspects of **software development lifecycle** (SDLC).

As applications become more data-centric, the interplay between software development, testing, and data management becomes even more critical. This evolving landscape introduces new challenges and considerations, hinting at the emergence of specialized methodologies like DataOps.

The software development method for a particular project will influence the choice of testing methodology. The two primary development approaches are briefly outlined here to facilitate deciding which direction a particular project will take.

Structure

The chapter covers the following topics:

- Traditional methodology
- Agile methodology
- Development
- Weighing the pros and cons
- Evolving role of data in software development
- Introduction to DataOps

Objectives

Testing is an indispensable component of the software development process. As IT professionals, adopting a test-driven mindset enables us to deliver higher-quality software through rapid feedback loops. In this chapter, we introduce the readers to **test-driven development** (**TDD**) methodology and contrast it with traditional testing approaches. Furthermore, we delve into the significance of data in modern software development and introduce the concept of DataOps, which emphasizes the importance of data operations in the agile development process.

Traditional methodology

The most common software development techniques are the **waterfall model, spiral model**, and **V model**. Though all of them have different concepts, they all have one thing in common, that is, the test is executed only after coding. The waterfall model is a sequential, linear approach to software design. The waterfall model is a strictly linear progression that moves through various stages, including conception, initiation, analysis, design, construction, testing, implementation, and maintenance. It is imperative to follow this process precisely to achieve optimal results. Any deviation from this model may lead to undesirable outcomes.

The waterfall methodology places significant emphasis on project planning, as it is crucial to have a precise plan and vision before commencing development. This approach's detailed planning allows the software to be launched quickly while providing greater accuracy in estimating budgets and timelines.

Agile methodology

The agile approach to software design is highly flexible, with adaptive planning and evolutionary development at its core. Agile is a freeform design model that involves developers working on small modules at a time. Throughout the development process, customer feedback and software testing happen simultaneously. This approach offers numerous benefits, particularly in project environments where development needs to be responsive and effective in the face of changing requirements.

This methodology promotes interaction and communication in software development, prioritizing collaboration over design to enable effective engagement between designers and stakeholders. It is especially beneficial in environments that emphasize teamwork. The development process involves multiple developers working on separate modules that are later integrated to produce a complete software product at the end of each iteration.

Development

In the dynamic world of software engineering, the term **development** encapsulates the processes, methodologies, and practices employed to bring software solutions to life. Development is a multifaceted journey from ideation to deployment that transforms requirements into functional software. Over the years, various approaches to development have emerged, each with its unique perspective on how software should be built and tested. Two prominent methodologies are **traditional development** and **TDD**. While the former emphasizes a sequential approach with testing following development, the latter intertwines testing with development, advocating for tests to be written even before the code itself.

Traditional development

A common practice in software development is to have an independent group of testers perform testing after the functionality is developed but before it is shipped to the customer. Refer to the following *Figure 1.1*:

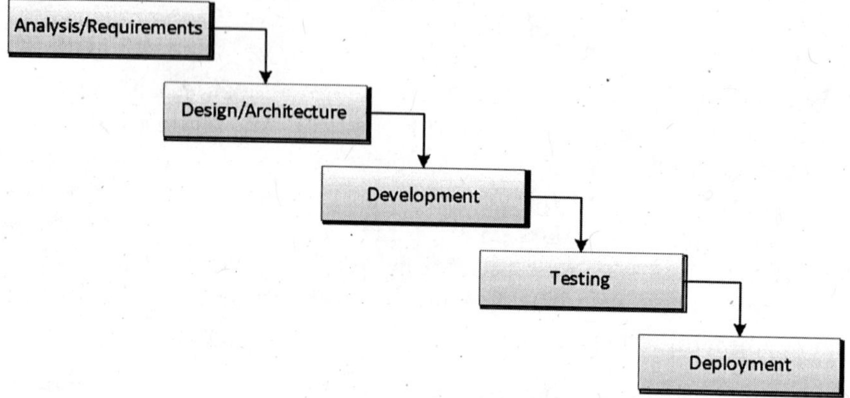

Figure 1.1: *Traditional development workflow*

Test-driven development

The initiation of software testing should commence at project commencement and endure until the ultimate completion phase. Refer to the following *Figure 1.2*:

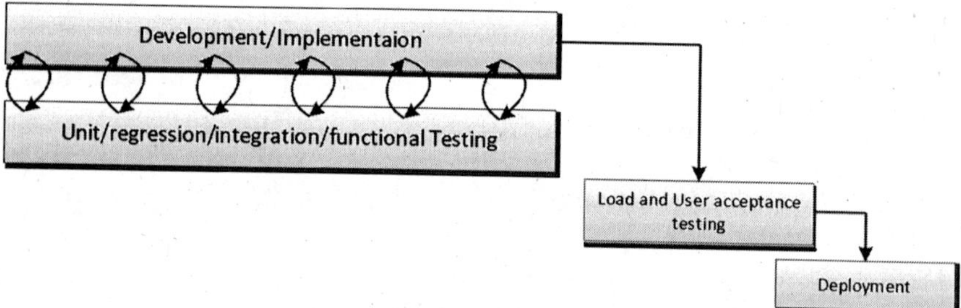

Figure 1.2: *TDD workflow*

Some software development methodologies, like Agile and Extreme programming, use a test-driven approach. Software engineers often write unit tests first. They frequently work in pairs and use the extreme programming method. At the start, engineers intentionally designed these tests to fail at first. However, as they write the code, it begins to pass. Over time, the code successfully meets more and more conditions of the test suites. The test suites are regularly updated with new failure conditions and corner cases and integrated with regression tests. Unit tests are maintained alongside the software code and integrated into the build process, with interactive tests being included in a partly manual build acceptance process. This testing process aims to enable continuous integration and frequent software updates to be released to the public. Engineering practices like TDD, continuous integration (continuous automated testing), constant refactoring, pair programming, frequent check-ins, and so on prevent technical dept.

This methodology increases the testing effort done by development before reaching any formal testing team. In some other development models, most test execution occurs after the requirements have been defined and the coding process has been completed.

Here is a simple flowchart that shows the different stages of the development cycle in a visual format. Refer to the following *Figure 1.3*:

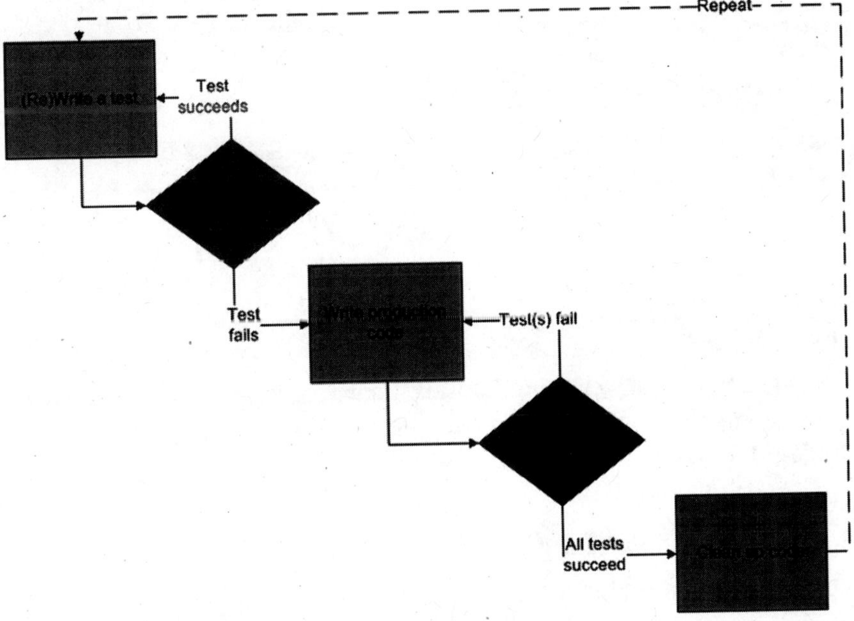

***Figure 1.3:** Different stages of the development cycle*

To get a holistic view of the sample environment, refer to the following *Figure 1.4*:

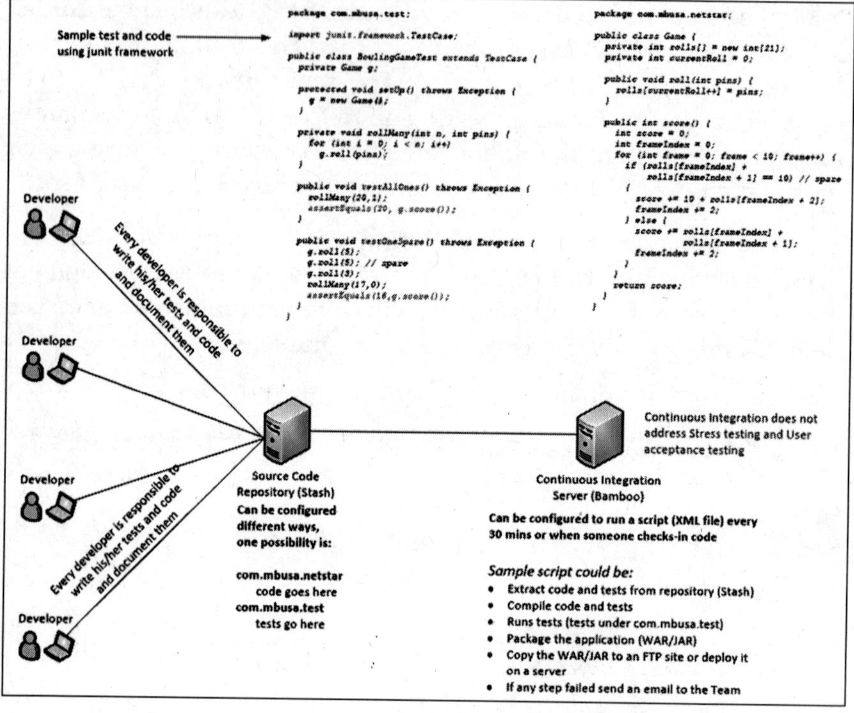

***Figure 1.4:** Sample environment*

Testing

Tests are frequently classified about their position within the software development process or their degree of specificity. The main levels during the development process are defined as:

- Unit testing
- Regression testing
- Integration testing
- Functional testing
- Security testing
- Load or stress testing
- User acceptance testing

TDD automates and enforces unit, regression, integration, security, and functional testing. It can be implemented successfully with a traditional development approach; however, when combined with agile software development frameworks, it allows the incorporation of load testing and user acceptance testing into the development cycle.

Weighing the pros and cons

Let us discuss the pros and cons of traditional development and TDD.

Pros

When evaluating software development approaches, it is helpful to consider the potential benefits of different methodologies. Understanding the advantages of traditional and TDD can provide insight into when each approach may be preferable.

Traditional development follows a sequential series of phases like requirements gathering, design, implementation, testing, and deployment. TDD focuses on iteratively writing tests before code, allowing the tests to drive incremental development.

Both methodologies have merits in certain situations.

Traditional development

The pros of traditional development include the following:

- Clear plan and a clear vision.
- You can launch software reasonably quickly.
- You can also estimate timetables and budgets more accurately.
- As the traditional methods require extensive planning and documentation, personnel turnover is less of a problem. A new designer/developer can quickly take over, following the development plan without a problem.

Test-driven development

The pros of TDD include the following:

- Using TDD can result in better-organized code, more adaptable and easier to expand.
- Performing numerous tests can effectively reduce the amount of defects present in the code. By conducting testing early and regularly, it is possible to detect defects during the development phase, preventing them from becoming widespread and costly. Addressing defects at an early stage of the process often eliminates the need for time-consuming and tedious debugging later in the project.
- Testing is not merely a final step in project development but a fundamental and essential component.

Cons

While traditional and TDD approaches have their advantages, they also come with some potential drawbacks to consider:

Traditional development follows a linear sequence that can lack the flexibility to change. TDD requires writing extensive test cases upfront, which can be time-consuming.

Understanding the cons of each methodology is vital for determining suitability.

Traditional development

The cons of the traditional approach involve the following:

- In instances of project delays, the act of testing is frequently forsaken as a means of creating a safety net.
- All requirements must be known upfront.
- No guarantee that the test written will be able to test the new functionality.
- The system has added unnecessary and repeated code that never executes.

Test-driven development

The cons of the TDD approach involve the following:

- Developers typically create unit tests in a TDD environment for their code. Suppose the developer misconstrues the requirements specification pertinent to the module being constructed. In that case, it is plausible that the code and accompanying tests may possess inadvertent blind spots, yielding a spurious impression of accuracy.
- The high number of passing unit tests can lead to reduced software testing activities, giving a false sense of security.
- Tests that are poorly written, such as those containing hard-coded error strings or being prone to failure, can become an expensive maintenance overhead for a project.

It is crucial for the success of TDD that the entire organization, including management, believes in its ability to improve the product. Otherwise, management may view time spent writing tests as wasted.

Evolving role of data in software development

As software development methodologies have evolved, so has the role of data in the development process. Real-time data processing, analytics, and **Machine Learning** (**ML**) techniques are critical for optimizing user experiences and increasing business value in modern applications. This shift has brought new challenges, especially when integrating data into the **continuous integration and continuous delivery** (**CI/CD**) process.

While effective for code, traditional software development and testing methodologies may need to address the unique challenges posed by data. Data is dynamic and often sourced from multiple origins, and its quality and integrity are paramount to the application's functionality. This increasing importance of data in software development necessitates specialized tools and practices to manage, test, and deploy data changes effectively.

Introduction to DataOps

DataOps, short for data operations, is an agile, process-oriented methodology designed to address these challenges. It promotes seamless collaboration between data engineers, scientists, and other operational teams. In an era where insights derived from data provide a competitive edge, traditional methods of handling data can lead to bottlenecks. DataOps emerges as a solution, ensuring data is readily available, reliable, and usable for analytics. Its significance lies in its ability to reduce the cycle time of data analytics, promote cross-functional collaboration, and ensure businesses to make informed decisions swiftly.

Definition and significance

DataOps, short for data operations, is an agile, process-oriented methodology designed to address these challenges. It promotes seamless collaboration between data engineers, scientists, and other operational teams. In an era where insights derived from data provide a competitive edge, traditional methods of handling data can lead to bottlenecks. DataOps emerges as a solution, ensuring data is readily available, reliable, and usable for analytics. Its significance lies in its ability to reduce the cycle time of data analytics, promote cross-functional collaboration, and ensure businesses make informed decisions swiftly.

DataOps in the context of TDD

TDD emphasizes writing tests before developing functionality, ensuring the software functions as intended. Similarly, DataOps places a strong emphasis on data quality and validation. Before any data is processed, predefined tests and validation checks are implemented to ensure accuracy and reliability. As TDD promotes rapid feedback loops for code changes, DataOps encourages continuous monitoring and validation of data, providing high-quality data for analytics and decision-making.

The intersection of DataOps and CI/CD

CI/CD focuses on automating the processes of integrating, testing, and deploying code changes. DataOps mirrors these principles but applies them to data. As data flows through various stages, from ingestion to processing to analytics, it undergoes automated tests and validations, ensuring it is always ready for analysis. DataOps can be viewed as the CI/CD equivalent for data, providing both application code and data are treated with the same rigor, discipline, and emphasis on quality.

Conclusion

In this introductory chapter, we embarked on a journey to understand the pivotal role of testing in the software development lifecycle. We delved deep into the essence of the TDD methodology, contrasting it with traditional testing approaches. The chapter highlighted the transformative power of rapid feedback loops in ensuring software quality. Furthermore, we explored the ever-evolving significance of data in today's software landscape, introducing the readers to the innovative concept of DataOps. This concept underscores the paramount importance of data operations within the agile development framework.

As we transition to the next chapter, we will dive deeper into the world of CI/CD. The upcoming chapter promises to unravel the core concepts of CI/CD and the emerging data CI/CD paradigm. Readers will gain insights into how these methodologies streamline software and data workflows and play a crucial role in ensuring software and data quality. So, gear up to delve into the intricacies of CI/CD and data CI/CD, and discover how they reshape the modern software and data development landscape.

CHAPTER 2
Understanding CI/ CD Concepts

Introduction

This chapter will delve into the world of **continuous integration (CI)**, including an introduction to data CI and its significance in data-driven applications. We explored the foundational concepts of CI and its significance in modern software development. Now, we shift our focus to the core practices, principles of continuous integration and continuous delivery, and how they emerged as a response to the challenges posed by traditional development practices. We will discuss the core principles behind **continuous integration and continuous delivery** (CI/CD), emphasizing the importance of frequent code integration, automation, and testing.

Structure

The chapter covers the following topics:

- Defining CI
- Role of CI / CD in software development
- Understanding continuous delivery
- Data CI / CD: The new frontier in data operations

- Benefits of CI/CD and data CI/CD
- Key attributes of data CI/CD
- CI/CD and data CI/CD workflow in action
- Integration with DevOps and DataOps
- CI/CD and data CI/CD tools and ecosystem
- Embracing a CI/CD and data CI/CD culture

Objectives

This chapter discusses the core principles of CI/CD. We will also introduce the emerging concept of data CI/CD. Readers will explore the benefits these practices bring to software and data workflows. While CI/CD emphasizes enhancing software quality, data CI/CD is dedicated to ensuring data integrity, quality, and reliability. By the end of this chapter, you will recognize the importance of both practices, understanding their pivotal role in modern software and data development to promote efficiency, collaboration, and overall quality.

Defining CI

Software that constantly crashes with bugs is unacceptable. Features that take forever to release are inefficient. CI addresses and resolves these issues! Your team's processes directly impact the efficiency of your software development workflow. Therefore, your team must adopt processes like CI that streamline your software development. CI automates code building and testing with each change, committing to a central repository. CI breaks down development tasks into smaller, manageable pieces to be regularly accomplished by the team. Whenever new code is committed, an automated build and test process, often called a **pipeline**, is triggered to identify any defects present during compilation or testing quickly. This approach aims to ensure consistency and efficiency in the development process. CI is one of the vital components of DevOps automation.

History and evolution of CI

CI emerged as a solution to the challenges posed by traditional development practices. In the past, long integration cycles and manual code merging led to bottlenecks and inconsistencies. CI introduced a paradigm shift by promoting frequent code integration and automation to streamline the development workflow.

Core principles of CI

At the heart of CI lie the following fundamental principles that underpin its effectiveness:

- **Frequent code integration:** Developers integrate their code changes multiple times daily, reducing integration issues and conflicts.
- **Automated build and test:** An automated build process compiles the code and generates executable artifacts whenever code changes are committed. After the build, automated tests are run to verify that the changes do not introduce regressions or bugs (combined build and test).
- **Rapid feedback loops:** The automated process provides developers with immediate feedback on the status of their code changes.
- **Maintain as single source repository:** All code and assets are stored in a version-controlled repository, ensuring consistency and traceability.
- **Keep the build fast:** The build process should be optimized as fast as possible, ensuring developers do not have to wait long to get feedback.
- **Test in a replicated production environment:** This ensures the code works in an environment like the production setup, reducing deployment issues.
- **Everyone commits to the mainline daily:** This ensures that developers are frequently integrating and not drifting too far from the main codebase.
- **Broken builds are prioritized:** If the build breaks, fixing it becomes the top priority, ensuring that issues are dealt with promptly and not postponed.

By using frequent code integrations and automated testing, CI improves software quality and speed of delivery.

Benefits of CI

By implementing CI, software development teams benefit from:

- **Easier bug fixes:** Identifying issues sooner makes it easier for developers to fix code errors, vulnerabilities, and defects. This helps to ensure that an issue will be fixed correctly, resulting in a build that is free of issues and works as quickly as possible.
- **Reduced project risk:** Encouraging small, modular changes to the code enables new functionality to be backed out of a release more quickly, or even prevented from entering the main code stream altogether. This minimizes the impact on other developers.
- **Improved software quality:** Maximizing the value of CI means detecting as many issues as possible in each integration build through automation. This increases the breadth, depth, and repeatability of the tests while avoiding manual testing.
- **Higher productivity:** Automating these tasks frees developers to focus on higher-value feature development.
- **Faster feedback:** Immediate feedback on code changes allows developers to catch and fix issues early, reducing the time spent on debugging.
- **Reduced integration issues:** Frequent code integration reduces the risk of integration conflicts and makes the integration process smoother.
- **Increased developer productivity:** CI automates repetitive tasks, freeing developers to focus on coding and innovation.
- **Enhanced collaboration:** CI encourages collaboration among team members, as everyone contributes to the shared codebase consistently.
- **Quick time-to-market:** Rapid code integration and testing enable faster delivery of new features and updates to end-users.

Role of CI/CD in software development

The **software development lifecycle (SDLC)** has been drastically improved by CI/CD. Traditionally, the SDLC was a linear and phased approach, where each stage of development, testing, and deployment happened sequentially. This often led to longer development cycles, delayed feedback, and a higher probability of errors during the integration phase.

With its emphasis on frequent code integrations, automated testing, and continuous feedback, CI/CD has transformed the SDLC into a more iterative and responsive process. No matter how minor, every code change goes through a rigorous automated process where it is integrated, tested, and made ready for deployment. This ensures that the software is always in a deployable state, significantly reducing the time between writing code and delivering it to the end-users.

Moreover, CI/CD bridges the gap between development and operations, leading to a more holistic approach to software delivery. CI/CD automates manual integration and deployment processes, ensuring continuous code flow from development to production, resulting in faster and more frequent software releases.

Maximize collaboration and productivity with CI/CD

One of the most profound impacts of CI/CD is on team collaboration and productivity. Before CI/CD, developers often worked in silos, integrating their code changes infrequently. This led to integration challenges, where merging code from different developers would result in conflicts and errors. Resolving these issues took time, leading to delays and reduced productivity.

CI/CD addresses this challenge head-on. Developers can quickly identify and rectify any issues by promoting frequent integrations and providing immediate feedback through automated tests. This reduces the time spent on debugging and fosters a culture of collaboration. Developers, testers, and operations staff work more closely, sharing real-time feedback and iterating on solutions.

Furthermore, CI/CD creates a transparent environment where every team member can see the development, testing, and deployment processes. This transparency fosters accountability and ensures everyone is aligned towards a common goal: delivering high-quality software quickly and efficiently.

In essence, CI/CD is the backbone of modern software development, promoting a culture of collaboration, continuous feedback, and rapid delivery. It ensures that teams are working hard and working smart, leveraging automation and best practices to deliver software that meets the highest standards of quality and reliability.

Understanding continuous delivery

Expecting flawless software only to encounter relentless bugs upon release is unacceptable. Wasted months on feature development due to quality issues is inefficient. Continuous delivery is the definitive solution. According to *Martin Fowler*, continuous delivery revolves around the notion that software is developed to fulfil business needs and must be delivered frequently and reliably. By ensuring faster delivery of working software, organizations can enable customers, both internal and external, to realize its benefits promptly. In a world where software plays a pivotal role in product offerings and service delivery, the ability to deliver software rapidly becomes critical for gaining a competitive edge.

Traditional approaches have limitations in that waterfall development methodologies often result in late and buggy software when attempts are made to speed up development cycles. Developers and IT professionals are understandably cautious about increasing the pace due to the limitations of traditional methods. The inability to test software frequently and thoroughly enough poses significant obstacles in delivering high-quality code.

To overcome the limitations of traditional approaches, continuous delivery incorporates several key principles and practices that streamline the software delivery process.

Let us explore these pillars:

- **Automation:** Automation makes successful processes repeatable and error-free. There is no need to worry about human mistakes from manual work. Whether introducing new features, adjusting infrastructure, or modifying services, automation handles software changes swiftly and flawlessly.
- **Frequent small code releases:** Continuous delivery processes software in smaller increments for a purpose. Instead of one giant yearly release, code is delivered in frequent small increments. This takes a bite-sized testing approach to catch

issues early before they compound. It also enables quick rollbacks if needed, reducing risk.

- **Comprehensive automated testing:** Comprehensive automated testing safeguards quality by preventing buggy code changes from moving down the pipeline. Only code that passes all defined tests can proceed to production. This **quality control** approach is essential for frequent releases.
- **Pull-based architecture:** An automated gatekeeper allows only perfectly tested code through to the next stage. By only allowing passing code changes to move forward, issues cannot snowball down the pipeline.
- **Cross-functional teams:** Isolated teams lead to fragmented software. Continuous delivery demands collaboration across disciplines: developers, testers, operations and so on. Together, these cross-functional teams release seamless, quality software by continuously sharing feedback and iterating.

By embracing these pillars, companies can pivot to reliably releasing high-quality updates users want frequently and rapidly.

With the right mindset, continuous delivery provides the recipe for satisfying users' software needs without leaving a bad taste from quality issues.

You're doing continuous delivery when:

Your software is deployable throughout its lifecycle.

Your team prioritizes keeping the software deployable over working on new features.

Anybody can get fast, automated feedback on the production readiness.

of their systems any time somebody makes a change to them

You can perform push-button deployments of any version of the software
to any environment on demand.

— Martin Fowler

Imagine a bustling kitchen where chefs continuously collaborate to prepare delicious dishes. There is a constant tasting of each other's culinary creations and feedback sharing to perfect every platter before it goes out to hungry diners.

That is an excellent analogy for continuous integration and delivery in software development.

CI mandates developers to consistently merge code changes into the primary repository, analogous to chefs incorporating ingredients into a meal. This initiates automatic tests, identifying issues promptly. By frequently integrating changes, conflicts are resolved swiftly, preventing further complications. This unifies all contributors, ensuring a cohesive output for optimal customer satisfaction. CD is contingent on this seamless integration. Transitioning to it also necessitates a departure from the outdated practice of releasing large annual software updates and the subsequent prolonged resolution of issues. Refer to the following *Figure 2.1*:

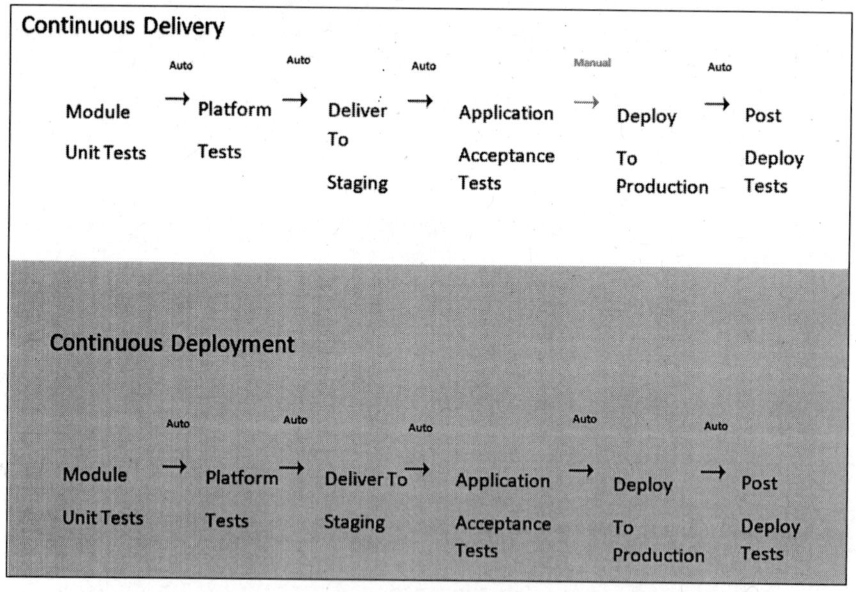

Figure 2.1: *Stages of continuous delivery and continuous deployment*

Software is developed, tested, and delivered in iterative cycles, ensuring frequent updates and feature enhancements. User feedback directly influences the trajectory of subsequent updates.

Both methodologies prioritize communication and collaboration. Immediate feedback loops transform errors and failures into opportunities for process improvement. Roles such as developers, testers, and operations share the responsibility for delivering and maintaining high-quality code.

Integration of technical teams is essential. Implement an environment that emphasizes continuous integration and automates testing to validate all changes.

The adoption of CI/CD principles leads to transformative results. Teams transition from isolated operations to a cohesive unit, delivering high-quality software. The frequency of quality issues diminishes as the development and delivery processes become more streamlined. In the realm of software operations, several esteemed authors have shed light on this topic. To provide a comprehensive understanding, following are some insights drawn from notable works:

Our highest priority is to satisfy the customer through early and continuous delivery of valuable software.

— First Principle, Agile Manifesto, 2001

You can't achieve really high levels of quality and verifiability in my experience by throwing things over the wall. The teams need to be working very, very closely together, communicating on a daily basis, interacting on tasks. So cross-functional teams all focused on delivering high quality software is the way to go.

— Dave Farley talking to Peter Bell of InfoQ

Data CI/CD: The new frontier in data operations

Data CI/CD is the next step for continuous integration and continuous delivery, designed for data workflows and operations. In the modern digital age, data has become an invaluable asset for organizations, driving decision-making, innovation, and competitive advantage. However, managing and deploying data changes can be as complex, if not more so, than managing software changes. Data CI/CD emerges as a solution to this challenge, ensuring that data workflows are as agile, reliable, and efficient as software workflows.

At its core, data CI/CD focuses on automating the integration, testing, and deployment of data changes. Whether it is new data being ingested into a system, updates to existing datasets, or changes to data processing pipelines, data CI/CD ensures that these changes are seamlessly integrated, validated, and deployed to production environments. This continuous flow ensures that data-driven applications always have access to the most accurate and up-to-date data.

Extending CI/CD principles to data workflows

Traditional CI/CD is rooted in the principles of frequent code integrations, automated testing, and continuous feedback. Data CI/CD takes these principles and adapts them to the unique challenges and nuances of data workflows. Let us see how data CI/CD extends traditional CI/CD principles:

- **Frequent data integrations:** Just as developers integrate code changes frequently in CI/CD, data CI/CD promotes the frequent integration of data changes. This could be new data sources being added, updates to existing data, or changes in data transformation logic. By integrating these changes frequently, organizations can ensure that their data pipelines are always current and reflective of the latest data.
- **Automated data testing:** Data quality is paramount. data CI/CD introduces automated testing for data, ensuring that any data changes meet the required quality standards. This could involve validating data formats, checking for missing values, or ensuring that data transformations produce the expected outputs. By automating these tests, organizations can catch and rectify data issues early in the pipeline, ensuring that only high-quality data reaches production environments.
- **Continuous feedback for data:** Data CI/CD provides continuous feedback on data changes. If a data integration fails or a data test does not pass, feedback is immediately relayed to the relevant teams. This rapid feedback loop ensures that data issues are addressed promptly, reducing the risk of faulty data impacting data-driven applications or decisions.

In essence, data CI/CD takes the best practices of traditional CI/CD and tailors them for the world of data. It recognizes that in today's data-centric world, data operations need to be as agile and reliable as software operations. By introducing automation, continuous feedback, and best practices to data workflows, data CI/CD is crucial for organizations to harness the full potential of their data assets in a seamless and efficient manner.

Benefits of CI/CD and data CI/CD

CI/CD has transformed software development by streamlining the process of development, testing, and deployment. Implementing CI/CD in software projects offers a myriad of advantages:

- **Faster release cycles:** CI/CD automates the software release process, enabling developers to deploy code changes more frequently and efficiently. Organizations can deliver new features and improvements to users faster with shorter release cycles.
- **Improved code quality:** With CI, every code change is automatically tested, ensuring that bugs and issues are identified and addressed early in the development process. This continuous testing ensures that the codebase remains stable and of high quality.
- **Enhanced collaboration:** CI/CD breaks down silos between development, testing, and operations teams. With a shared responsibility for code quality and deployment, teams collaborate more effectively, leading to better outcomes.
- **Reduced deployment risks:** By deploying smaller changes more frequently, the risks associated with deployments are significantly reduced. If an issue arises, it is easier to identify and rectify, minimizing disruptions.
- **Immediate feedback:** Developers receive immediate feedback on their code changes, allowing them to address issues in real time. This rapid feedback loop fosters a culture of continuous improvement.

Impact of data CI/CD on data analytics projects

Data CI/CD significantly reshapes data analytics projects, offering many benefits. It automates data changes integration, testing, and deployment, ensuring that data workflows are efficient and reliable. This automation reduces manual interventions, leading to faster and more consistent data operations.

Automated data CI/CD testing ensures that data meets the required quality standards. Whether validating data formats, checking for anomalies, or ensuring data consistency, data CI/CD ensures that data-driven projects are built on high-quality data.

Just as CI/CD brings agility to software development, data CI/CD brings agility to data operations. Data teams can quickly adapt to changing data sources, update data transformations, and deploy new data models, ensuring that analytics projects remain current and relevant.

Data CI/CD fosters collaboration between data scientists, engineers, and business stakeholders. With a shared responsibility for data quality and deployment, teams work together more effectively, leading to better data-driven insights.

In the dynamic world of data, sources can change, and data can drift over time. Data CI/CD provides:

- Continuous monitoring and feedback.
- Ensuring that data drift is identified and addressed promptly.
- Maintaining the integrity of data science and analytics projects.

In conclusion, CI/CD and data CI/CD are transformative approaches that bring efficiency, quality, and agility to software and data projects. By embracing these methodologies, organizations can harness the full potential of their software and data assets, driving innovation and competitive advantage.

Key attributes of data CI/CD

Software development and data operations have been transformed by the principles of CI, CD data CI/CD. While distinct in their nuances, these methodologies share core attributes that drive their success. Let us delve into these key attributes and understand their significance.

The characteristics of data CI/CD are as follows:

- **Automated testing:** One of the foundational attributes of CI/CD is the automation of testing. Every code or data change is automatically tested to ensure it does not introduce errors or regressions. This ensures that the code or data is always in a deployable state.
- **Frequent integrations:** CI emphasizes integrating code changes frequently, often multiple times a day. This ensures that changes are minor, making them easier to test and deploy and reducing the chances of merge conflicts.

- **Automated deployments:** Continuous delivery and continuous deployment take CI further by automating the deployment process. While CD ensures that code is always in a deployable state, continuous deployment goes the extra mile by automatically deploying every change that passes the automated tests.
- **Version control:** All changes, whether to code or data are tracked in version control systems. This provides a history of changes, facilitates collaboration among team members, and allows for easy rollbacks if needed.
- **Infrastructure as Code: Infrastructure as Code** (**IaC**) manages and provides infrastructure through code, ensuring the environment is consistent, reproducible, and scalable.
- **Feedback loops:** CI/CD methodologies prioritize rapid feedback. Developers and data teams are notified if their changes pass or fail the automated tests, allowing quick corrections.
- **Collaboration and communication:** CI/CD fosters a culture of collaboration and open communication among developers, operations, testing teams, and other stakeholders. It is crucial to ensure everyone works together towards a shared objective.

Attributes for efficient software and data operations

The attributes of CI, CD, and data CI/CD are not just theoretical concepts; they have practical implications that ensure efficiency and reliability in software and data operations:

- **Reduced errors:** Automated testing and frequent integrations mean errors are caught early and easier to fix. This reduces the chances of bugs making their way into the production environment.
- **Faster time to market:** Automated deployments and streamlined workflows mean new features, improvements, and fixes can be delivered to users more quickly.
- **Consistency:** With IaC and version control, every environment, whether development, testing, or production, is consistent. This reduces the it works on my machine problems and ensures that code runs reliably in any environment.

- **Scalability:** Automated workflows, IaC, and other CI/CD attributes ensure that operations can scale to meet the demands of growing user bases and increasing data volumes.
- **Enhanced collaboration:** With clear communication channels and collaborative practices, teams can work together more effectively, leading to better outcomes and faster problem resolution.

In essence, the critical attributes of continuous integration, delivery, deployment, and data CI/CD are the pillars that support efficient, reliable, and agile software and data operations. To outperform competitors and attain operational excellence, organizations must adopt these attributes.

CI/CD and data CI/CD workflow in action

The CI/CD and data CI/CD workflows have revolutionized how software and data projects are managed, tested, and deployed. These workflows are designed to automate and streamline processes, ensuring that software and data are always deployable. Let us explore these workflows in detail and understand them through real-world examples.

A step-by-step walkthrough of a typical CI/CD pipeline is as follows:

1. **Version control commit:** Developers make changes to the code or data and commit these changes to a version control system like **Git**. This is the starting point of the CI/CD pipeline.
2. **Automated build:** The CI/CD system automatically triggers a build process once changes are committed. This involves compiling the code, packaging it, and preparing it for deployment.
3. **Automated testing:** After the build, automated tests are run. These tests can range from unit tests, which test individual components of the software, to integration tests, which test the software as a whole.
4. **Deployment to staging:** The code is deployed to a staging environment once the tests have passed. This environment closely mirrors the production environment and is used for final testing before deployment.

5. **Manual review:** In some workflows, especially continuous delivery, there is a manual review step where stakeholders can review the changes in the staging environment.
6. **Deployment to production:** After verifying everything, the code is deployed to the production environment to make the changes live for users.
7. **Monitoring and feedback:** The application and data processes are continuously monitored after deployment. Any issues or feedback are used to inform future changes, creating a feedback loop.

Real-world examples of CI/CD and data CI/CD

Let us look at some of the real-world examples where implementing CI/CD has been a huge help to the businesses:

Example 1: Software development at Netflix

Netflix, the global streaming giant, is known for its extensive use of CI/CD. They deploy code changes thousands of times daily using their custom-built **Spinnaker** platform. This remarkable deployment frequency enables Netflix to rapidly roll out new features, bug fixes, and optimizations to its streaming service. By doing so, they maintain a seamless and responsive user experience for millions of subscribers worldwide. This approach aligns perfectly with their customer-centric philosophy, as they continuously strive to enhance their platform.

Example 2: Data CI/CD at Airbnb

Airbnb, a leading platform for home-sharing and travel experiences, has successfully applied CI/CD principles to its data workflows. They leverage a tool called **Apache Airflow** to manage their intricate data pipelines. Data CI/CD practices are integral to their data operations, ensuring that data is consistently processed, transformed, and made readily available to data scientists and analysts. This streamlined data pipeline guarantees that Airbnb can extract valuable insights from its vast data repository, enhancing its services and user experiences.

Example 3: E-commerce at Etsy

Etsy, a prominent online marketplace for handmade and unique goods, has established a robust CI/CD pipeline. Their commitment to agile development is evident in their deployment of code changes more than 50 times daily. This impressive deployment frequency empowers Etsy to adapt to shifts in the e-commerce landscape swiftly, introduce new features, and optimize buyers' and sellers' overall user experience. By embracing CI/CD, Etsy remains competitive and can readily respond to market changes and customer demands.

In conclusion, adopting CI/CD and data CI/CD workflows has become a cornerstone of success across various industries. These methodologies have proven to be powerful tools, enhancing organizations' agility, efficiency, and responsiveness. Automating and streamlining processes guarantees that software and data are consistently of high quality and always in a deployable state. These real-world examples underscore the transformative impact of CI/CD practices, driving innovation and excellence in diverse sectors and industries.

Integration with DevOps and DataOps

In the ever-evolving landscape of software development and data management, DevOps, DataOps, and CI/CD concepts have emerged as transformative methodologies. They aim to enhance collaboration, streamline processes, and deliver high-quality products swiftly. Let us delve into the intricate relationship between these concepts and understand how they complement each other.

Understanding CI/CD, DevOps, and DataOps Relationships DevOps is a movement that emphasizes collaboration between development and operations teams, both culturally and technically. It seeks to bridge the traditional silos, ensuring faster delivery of applications and services. At its core, DevOps is about automating and optimizing the software development lifecycle.

DataOps, on the other hand, is a similar philosophy but applied to data analytics. It focuses on improving communication between data professionals and operations, ensuring data is reliable, accessible, and ready for analysis.

CI/CD is a set of practices that ensure code changes are tested and deployed automatically, enabling frequent releases and rapid feedback.

While DevOps and DataOps provide the overarching philosophy and culture, CI/CD offers the practical tools and processes to realize these principles. CI/CD pipelines are the backbone of DevOps and DataOps, automating the steps from code commit to production deployment.

CI/CD's role in DevOps and DataOps CI/CD serves as the backbone of modern software development, enhancing both DevOps and DataOps practices. Its contributions are evident in the following key areas that underscore the importance of streamlined development and operational workflows:

- **Automation:** One of the primary tenets of DevOps and DataOps is automation. CI/CD pipelines automate the build, test, and deployment processes, reducing manual intervention and potential errors. This automation ensures consistent and rapid delivery.
- **Collaboration:** CI/CD fosters collaboration by providing developers, testers, and operations teams with a shared platform. With tools like version control and automated testing, teams can work together seamlessly, ensuring that code is always in a deployable state.
- **Feedback loops:** CI/CD pipelines provide immediate feedback. Developers are instantly notified if a build fails or a test does not pass. This rapid feedback loop aligns with the DevOps and DataOps principles of continuous improvement.
- **Flexibility and scalability:** As organizations grow, so do their development and data needs. CI/CD pipelines can be scaled to accommodate larger teams and more complex projects, ensuring that the principles of DevOps and DataOps can be applied regardless of the organization's size.
- **Quality assurance:** With CI/CD, every code change is tested before deployment. This rigorous testing ensures the software is high quality and free from critical issues. It aligns with the DevOps and DataOps goal of delivering reliable and robust products.

In conclusion, CI/CD is not just a set of tools or practices but an integral part of the DevOps and DataOps philosophies. By integrating CI/CD into their workflows, organizations can harness the power of collaboration, automation, and continuous improvement, leading to unparalleled efficiency and innovation.

CI/CD and data CI/CD tools and ecosystem

Transitioning from traditional CI/CD to a more data-centric approach requires understanding the tools that power these processes. Before diving into the specifics of popular CI/CD tools, it is essential to recognize the broader ecosystem and how data CI/CD tools fit within it.

Overview of popular CI/CD tools

The following are the popular CI/CD tools, discussed in detail:

- **Jenkins:** Jenkins, often revered as the gold standard in CI/CD, is an open-source automation server known for its robustness and extensibility. It boasts a rich history and a vibrant community that continually contributes to its development. Jenkins stands out with its vast plugin ecosystem, offering an unmatched level of flexibility. Teams can harness Jenkins to automate every phase of the development cycle. This includes code compilation, automated testing, and seamless deployment, making Jenkins a comprehensive solution for CI/CD. Its adaptability and customizability empower organizations to tailor their CI/CD pipelines precisely to their unique requirements.
- **Travis CI:** Travis CI is a cloud-based CI/CD service that has gained widespread acclaim, particularly for its seamless integration with GitHub repositories. This integration makes it exceptionally user-friendly, as it automatically detects when a commit or pull request is made to a GitHub repository and swiftly triggers the associated tests and builds. Travis CI excels in simplicity and ease of setup, making it a preferred choice for many developers, especially those engaged in open-source projects. It offers a hassle-free and effective means of automating testing and deployments, ensuring code quality and reliability.
- **CircleCI:** CircleCI is another prominent cloud-based CI/CD platform contender. What sets CircleCI apart is its focus on

providing a streamlined experience for developers. It offers features such as Docker support, allowing teams to create containerized environments for testing and deployment. CircleCI facilitates intricate workflow configurations and supports matrix builds, enabling teams to parallelize tasks effectively. Its intuitive user interface and robust performance metrics empower development teams to deliver high-quality code at an accelerated pace. CircleCI's flexibility and scalability make it an excellent choice for organizations aiming to optimize and streamline their CI/CD processes.

Introduction to tools specific to data CI/CD

The following tools are specific to data CI/CD process:

- **Data Version Control:** In the data CI/CD domain, **Data Version Control** (DVC) emerges as a crucial open-source tool designed explicitly for machine learning projects. DVC equips data scientists and machine learning practitioners with the ability to version datasets, machine learning models, and intermediate files. DVC integrates seamlessly with Git, aligning data management with familiar version control workflows. This seamless integration ensures that teams can efficiently manage code and data, contributing to the reproducibility and integrity of machine learning workflows. DVC becomes indispensable for maintaining data consistency and facilitating collaboration among data science teams.
- **Great expectations:** Great expectations is a specialized tool that plays a pivotal role in data CI/CD by focusing on data testing, documentation, and profiling. It empowers data teams to articulate and enforce data quality and consistency expectations. By setting stringent criteria for data validation, great expectations ensures that data-driven projects are constructed on a robust foundation of high-quality data. This tool aids in maintaining data integrity, reliability, and adherence to predefined standards across diverse data sources.
- **Pachyderm:** Pachyderm is a comprehensive platform tailored to address the intricate challenges associated with data CI/CD. It offers version-controlled, automated, and reproducible data pipelines, enabling teams to manage data

integration, transformation, and deployment efficiently. With Pachyderm, tracking changes in data and code becomes seamless, simplifying the maintenance and scalability of data workflows. Its holistic approach ensures that data operations remain reliable, well-organized, and conducive to agile data management.

- **data build tool:** The **data build tool (dbt)**, caters to data analysts and engineers working within data warehouses. This tool empowers teams to execute data transformations and modeling, emphasizing version control, testing, and documentation. By adopting dbt organizations can ensure that data transformations are reliable and comprehensively documented, promoting transparency and accountability. dbt contributes significantly to enhanced data quality, integrity, and the facilitation of data-driven decision-making processes.

In summary, the CI/CD ecosystem offers various tools designed to cater to the diverse needs of software developers and data professionals. These tools allow organizations to automate critical processes, enhance quality, and streamline workflows. Furthermore, as the landscape of CI/CD and data CI/CD continues to evolve, the development of increasingly specialized tools is anticipated. These tools will further simplify and enhance CI/CD processes, reaffirming their vital role in modern software and data development practices.

Embracing a CI/CD and data CI/CD culture

Embracing a CI/CD and data CI/CD culture goes beyond merely implementing tools and setting up pipelines. It is about fostering an environment where continuous integration, delivery, and deployment become integral to the organization's ethos. This cultural shift is pivotal for organizations aiming to stay agile, competitive, and responsive to the ever-evolving market demands.

It cannot be emphasized enough how crucial it is to cultivate a culture that embraces the principles of CI/CD. A culture that values CI/CD prioritizes collaboration, transparency, and feedback. It is a culture where developers, testers, operations teams, and data professionals work together, breaking down silos and ensuring that code and data flow smoothly from one stage to the next. Such a culture recognizes that failures are learning opportunities, and rapid iterations lead to superior products and solutions.

Transitioning to a CI/CD and data CI/CD mindset is challenging. Organizations must rethink their traditional workflows and embrace a more iterative and collaborative approach.

Here are some tips for organizations looking to make this transition:

- **Leadership buy-in:** The journey to CI/CD starts at the top. Leaders must understand the value of CI/CD and champion its adoption throughout the organization.
- **Continuous learning:** Encourage teams to stay updated with the latest CI/CD practices and tools. Regular training sessions and workshops can be invaluable.
- **Feedback loops:** Establish mechanisms for continuous feedback. Whether through automated tests, code reviews, or post-deployment monitoring, feedback helps teams iterate and improve.
- **Collaborative environment:** Foster an environment where teams collaborate freely. Encourage open communication and ensure that teams have the tools to collaborate effectively.
- **Celebrate successes and learn from failures:** Recognize and reward teams that embrace CI/CD principles. At the same time, create a safe space where teams can discuss failures and learn from them.

In conclusion, embracing a CI/CD and data CI/CD culture is a transformative journey that offers immense benefits. Organizations that successfully make this transition enjoy faster release cycles, improved product quality, and enhanced team collaboration. It is a journey worth undertaking for those looking to stay at the forefront of technological innovation.

Conclusion

This chapter has addressed the fundamentals and intricacies of CI/CD. We established the paramount role of CI/CD in the development lifecycle and introduced data CI/CD as a critical evolution in data operations. The benefits and key attributes of these practices stand evident. Through practical demonstrations, we underscored the integration of CI/CD and data CI/CD with DevOps and DataOps.

The tools and ecosystems supporting CI/CD and data CI/CD are indispensable for modern development. It is imperative for organizations to embed a CI/CD and data CI/CD culture to achieve technological excellence.

As we transition to the next chapter, we will focus on the construction of an efficient CI/CD pipeline, a cornerstone of modern software development. We will delve into the meticulous process of building a resilient pipeline, exploring stages from its inception to the orchestration of containerized applications. Topics such as CI pipeline construction, Jenkins implementation, automation testing strategies, containerization, version control, and IaC will be at the forefront of our discussion.

CHAPTER 3

Building the CI/CD Pipeline

Introduction

This chapter delves deep into the intricacies of **continuous integration and continuous delivery** (**CI/CD**) and data CI/CD, emphasizing their pivotal role in contemporary software development. We will guide you through crafting a resilient CI/CD pipeline that integrates code and ensures seamless data delivery. From the initial stages of code writing and testing to the final product delivery, we illuminate the critical elements that bolster code quality, uniformity, and swift deployment. By harnessing the power of this comprehensive system, development teams can significantly reduce manual interventions, leading to minimized errors and expedited results. With the added dimension of data CI/CD, we ensure that applications are always fueled by the most current and accurate data, enhancing overall productivity.

Structure

The chapter covers the following topics:

- Constructing a continuous integration pipeline
- Stages of CI/CD pipeline
- Implementation with Jenkins

- Automation testing strategies
- Data integration in CI/CD
- Data validation and testing
- Data deployment strategies
- Data rollback mechanisms
- Containerization and orchestration
- Version control and source management
- Infrastructure as Code

Objectives

After understanding CI/CD and data CI/CD in this chapter, let us learn about setting up a continuous integration pipeline. When combined with agile concepts, a well-designed CI/CD pipeline can smooth the software development process, leading to better-quality software delivered more quickly. The main goal of a CI/CD pipeline is to automate the entire software development process, including the integration and delivery of data.

We will learn about various parts of the software development process, like writing code, running tests, and delivering the final product. The CI/CD pipeline is a way to bring automation and continuous monitoring into this development cycle. It includes all the stages of the software development process and connects them, making it easier to manage and streamline the whole process. This entire setup is known as a **CI/CD pipeline**.

Using this system will decrease the manual work for the development team, which means fewer mistakes and faster outcomes. These improvements will lead to a more productive delivery team overall. With the inclusion of data CI/CD, teams can also ensure that data is integrated seamlessly, ensuring that applications always use the most up-to-date and accurate data.

Constructing a continuous integration pipeline

The main reason for using CI/CD is to help teams get quick, correct, dependable, and complete feedback during their development process. So, a promising pipeline should focus on these factors: speed, accuracy, reliability, and understanding.

Key characteristics

The following are the key characteristics of a good CI/CD pipeline:

- **Speed:** CI aims to be fast, providing immediate feedback to developers. If it takes more than 10 minutes to verify their build in the **quality assurance** (**QA**) environment, it disrupts them because they have to wait and switch between tasks.

  In a CI/CD pipeline, the time it takes for each code change affects how often developers can deploy daily updates. Businesses must update quickly and adapt to changes, so the engineering team requires a CI/CD process supporting a fast workflow.

  As the business grows, the CI/CD tools must be able to scale quickly to meet new demands. A good tool should be programmable and fit into the existing development workflows. The CI/CD configuration should also be stored as codes for review, versioning, and future use.

- **Accuracy:** Using automation in the deployment process is a good beginning, but more than automation is needed to create a valuable and effective CI/CD pipeline. Along with other tools, the pipeline needs to correctly manage simple and complex workflows, avoiding mistakes in repetitive tasks.

  The more precise the pipeline is, the closer it comes to being completely automated from continuous integration to continuous deployment without human intervention.

- **Reliability:** A dependable CI/CD pipeline makes building and deploying new code changes much faster. The pipeline should always produce consistent results without fluctuations in performance.

  As mentioned before, the CI/CD infrastructure needs to handle the increasing demands of the product team. As the number of teams and projects grows or the workflow changes, the pipeline should remain reliable and capable of supporting the increased workload.

- **Comprehension:** A promising CI/CD pipeline should include all the different parts of the software delivery process. If even one phase is left out in the CI/CD tools, it can significantly impact the whole pipeline.

Examples of CI/CD pipeline workflows

Now, let us see how two CI/CD pipelines work. The first is a traditional pipeline, and then we will check out a cloud-based one.

Traditional CI/CD pipeline

The following pipeline represents a simple web application development process in *Figure 3.1*:

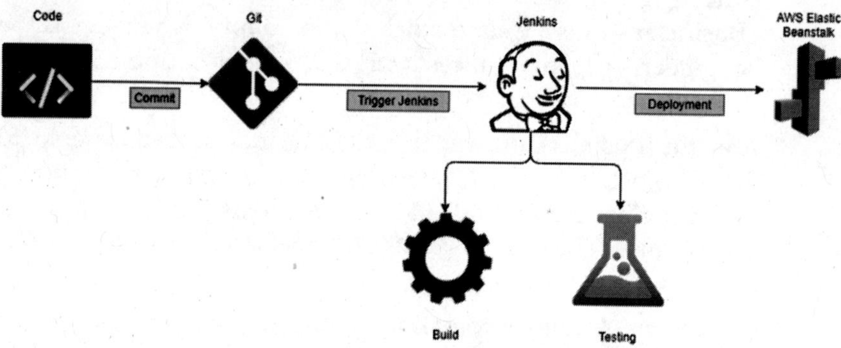

Figure 3.1: *Traditional CI/CD pipeline workflow*

Here is how the actual pipeline works. The developer writes and saves the code in a central repository:

- When the report detects a change, it triggers the Jenkins server.
- Jenkins takes the new code, automatically builds it, and runs tests. Jenkins informs the development team through email or Slack if any issues are found.
- The final package is deployed for production to AWS Elastic Beanstalk, an orchestration service.
- The Elastic Beanstalk handles infrastructure provisioning, load balancing, and scaling of various resource types, such as **Elastic Compute Cloud** (**EC2**) and RDS.

  This is a good example, but yours can be different. The tools, steps, and complexity of a CI/CD pipeline will be based on what the organization needs for development and business. The outcome could be either:

  - A simple four-stage pipeline.
  - A complex pipeline with multiple stages running together, including various builds, different types of tests (like

smoke test, regression test, and user acceptance testing), and deploying to different platforms (like web and mobile).

Cloud-based CI/CD pipeline

As more people use cloud technologies, the current trend is to do DevOps tasks in the cloud. Providers like Azure and AWS offer complete services to handle all the needed DevOps tasks using their platforms.

The following figure is a straightforward cloud-based DevOps CI/CD pipeline that uses Azure tools (Azure DevOps services):

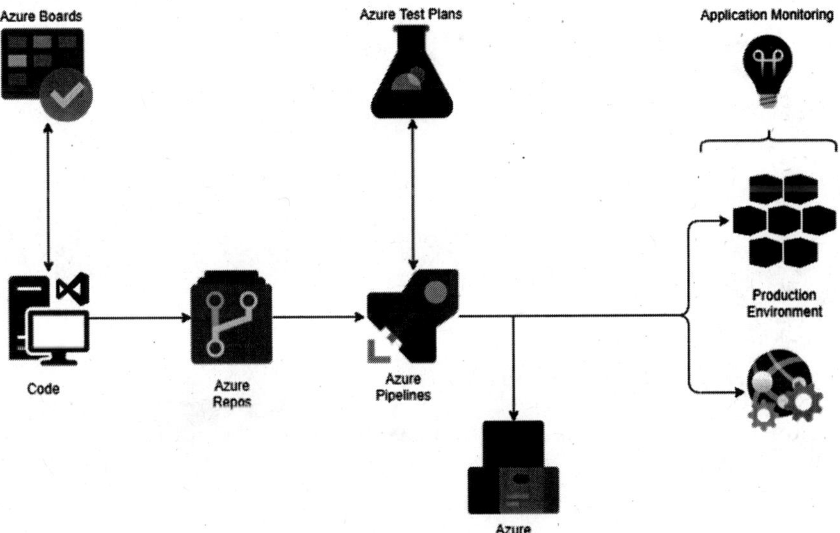

Figure 3.2: *Cloud based CI/CD pipeline workflow*

Here is how an actual cloud-based CI/CD pipeline works:

- A developer creates or modifies source code and then commits to Azure repos.
- These repo changes trigger the Azure Pipeline.
- When new code changes are made, Azure Test Plans and Azure Pipelines work together to build and test the code in a continuous integration process.
- Azure Pipelines trigger the deployment of tested and built artifacts to required environments with dependencies and variables. (continuous deployment)
- Artifacts are stored in the Azure artifacts service, a universal repository.

- Azure's application monitoring services provide developers real-time insights into the deployed applications. These insights include health reports and usage information, which can help developers understand their applications' behavior.

In addition to the CI/CD pipeline, Azure offers Azure Boards as an agile planning tool for managing the **software development lifecycle** (**SDLC**). There are two options available for users:

- Manually configure a complete CI/CD pipeline.
- Choose a SaaS solution like Azure DevOps or DevOps tooling by AWS.

Stages of CI/CD pipeline

A CI/CD pipeline is divided into six main stages:

1. Source
2. Build
3. Test
4. Deployment
5. Automated testing phase
6. Deploy to the production phase.

Before moving on to the next stage, each step must be finished first. We keep a close eye on all the stages to check for mistakes or differences, and then we give feedback to the delivery team.

In an Agile environment, every development task, whether bug fixing or adding a new feature, goes through the CI/CD pipeline before it is released to the public.

This system will make things easier for the development team, meaning fewer mistakes and faster results. All of this together helps the delivery team work more efficiently. Refer to the following *Figure 3.3*:

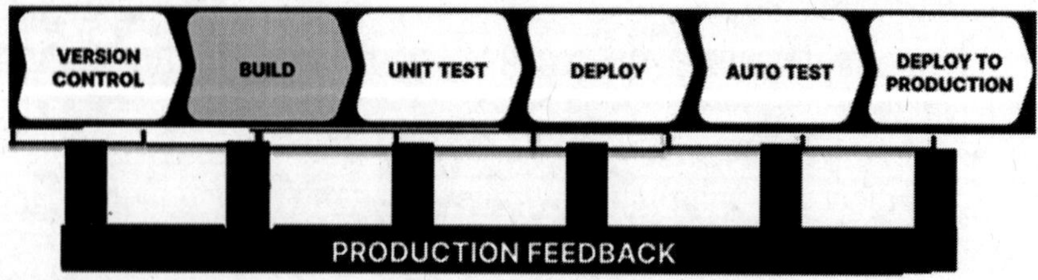

Figure 3.3: *Stages of a CI/CD pipeline*

Let us discuss the stages in detail:

1. **Source stage:** This is the initial step in the CI/CD pipeline. In this stage, the pipeline starts whenever there is a change in the program or when a specific signal is set in the code repository (repo). This stage deals with source control, which involves managing different code versions and keeping track of changes.

   In this stage, if there is any change in the main repository (like a new commit or version), the automated process will start tasks like compiling the code and running unit tests.

   Typical tools in the source stage include:

   - Git
   - SVN
   - Azure Repos
   - AWS CodeCommit

2. **Build stage:** In the second stage of the pipeline, the source code is put together with all its dependencies to create a version of the software that can be run or executed. This stage includes (list of specific tasks or processes covered in the stage):

   - Software builds
   - Other kinds of buildable objects, for example Docker containers.

   This stage is the most crucial one. If there is a problem in the build process, it could be a fundamental issue in the code.

   Moreover, in this stage, we also handle the build artifacts. We store these artifacts centrally, using yarn or a cloud-based solution like Azure Artifacts. This way, we can go back to the previous build if there are any problems with the current one.

   Tools that support the build stage:

   - Jenkins
   - Travis CI
   - Gradle
   - Azure Pipelines
   - AWS Code Build

3. **Test stage:** In the test stage, we use automated testing to check if the software works correctly. The main aim is to catch any

bugs before the users encounter them. Different types of testing, like integration and functional testing, are done in this stage. It helps us find and fix any mistakes in the product.

Standard test tools include:

- Selenium
- PHPUnit
- Jest
- Appium
- Puppeteer
- Playwright

4. **Deploy stage:** This is the last stage of the pipeline. The package is ready to deploy once everything has passed the earlier stages. We do this in two steps: first, to a staging environment for additional QA, and then to the actual production environment. This stage can be adjusted to work with different deployment strategies, such as (list of deployment strategies):

   - In-place deployments
   - Blue-green deployments
   - Canary deployments

   In the deployment stage, we set up the necessary infrastructure, configured everything correctly, and used technologies like Docker, Puppet, Terraform, and Kubernetes. Other tools include:

   - Chef
   - Ansible
   - AWS Code Deploy
   - Azure Pipelines – Deployment
   - AWS Elastic Beanstalk

5. **Automation stage:** The automation test phase is the last step, where we do the final tests to check if the built features are good enough to be released to users. We use automated and continuous testing to test the builds and ensure no bugs are left before deploying the software to production.

   During the entire pipeline, if there is an error, the development team will quickly receive feedback to fix the issues immediately.

After making the necessary code changes to address the bugs, the fixed code will go through the production pipeline again.

6. **Deploy to the production stage:** Once the codes or the product passes all the tests without issues, they are ready to go to the production server in the last phase. The constant feedback loop makes the pipeline a closed process where builds are regularly tested, and once they pass, they are deployed to production.

Implementation with Jenkins

Let us demonstrate how to set up a basic CI/CD pipeline using Jenkins in this section.

Before starting, make sure to configure Jenkins with all the necessary dependencies. It is also important to have a basic understanding of Jenkins concepts. In this example, Jenkins is set up in a Windows environment. Let us cover the steps in detail:

1. **Accessing Jenkins:** First, log in to Jenkins and select **New Item**. Refer to the following *Figure 3.4*:

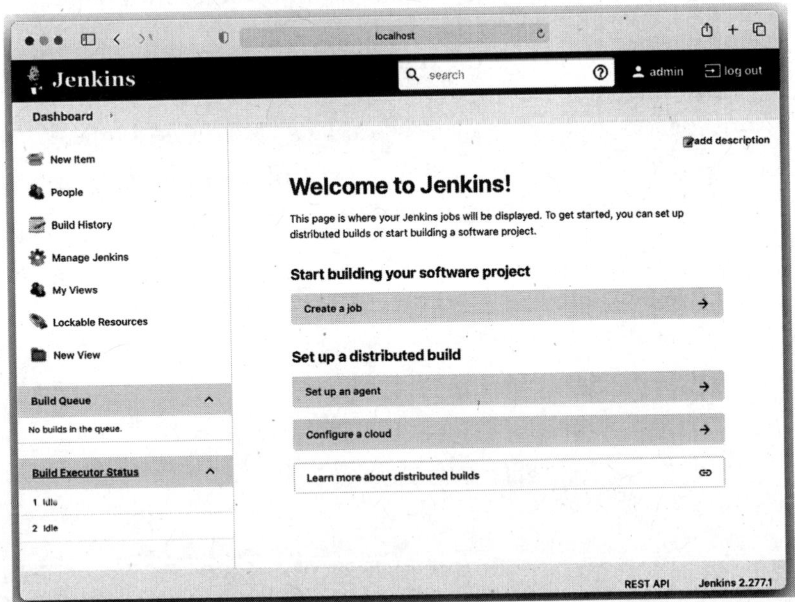

***Figure 3.4:** Accessing Jenkins*

2. **Naming the pipeline:** Choose **Pipeline** from the menu and give the pipeline a name. Click **OK** to proceed. Refer to the following *Figure 3.5*:

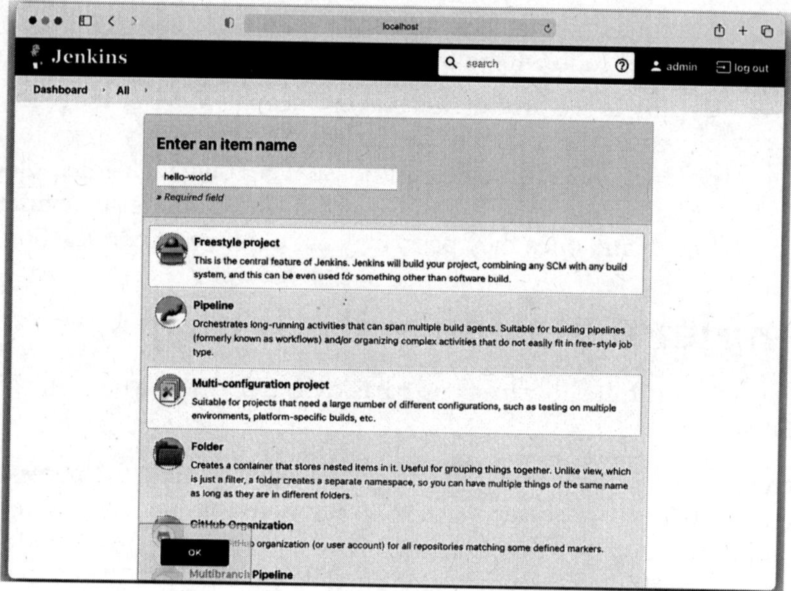

Figure 3.5: Naming the pipeline

3. **Configuring the pipeline:** You can configure the pipeline on its configuration screen. Here, you can set build triggers and various options for the pipeline. The section where you define the stages of the pipeline is called **Pipeline Definition**. The pipeline supports both declarative and scripted syntaxes.

   In this example, we will use a sample **`Hello World`** pipeline script. Consider the code below:

```
pipeline {
    agent any
    stages {
        stage ('Hello') {
            steps {
                echo 'Hello World'
                }
                }
            }
        }
```

   Once you have configured the pipeline, the next step is to set build triggers and various options for the pipeline, as shown in the following figure:

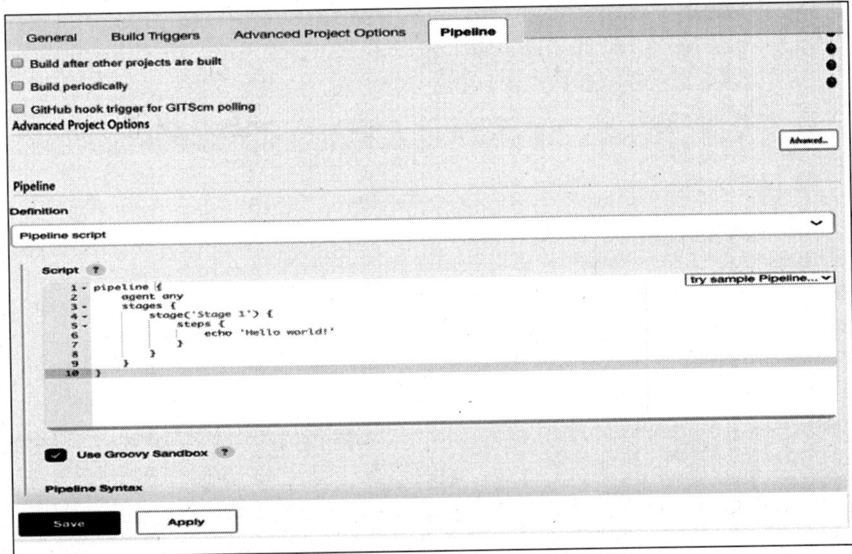

Figure 3.6: Configuring the pipeline

Click on **Apply** and **Save**. You have completed the configuration of a simple pipeline successfully.

4. **Executing the pipeline:** To initiate the pipeline, simply click on the **Build Now** button. Refer to the following *Figure 3.7*:

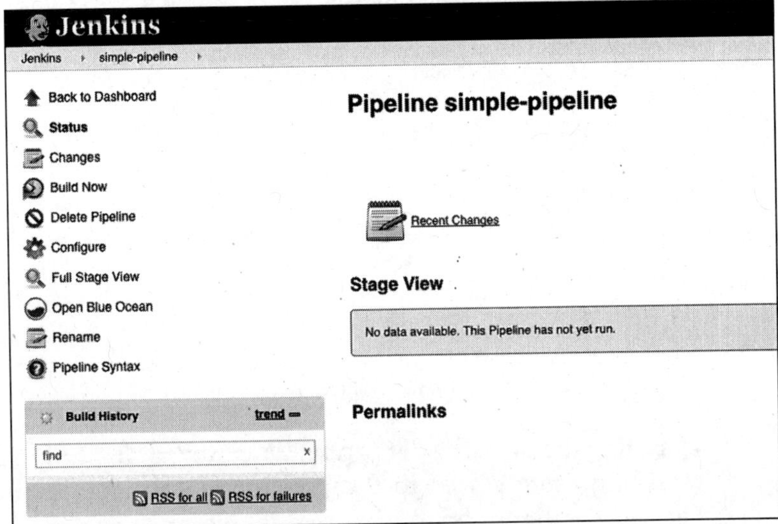

Figure 3.7: Executing the pipeline

You will observe that the various stages of the pipeline will begin to execute, and the results will be shown in the **Stage**

View section. It should be noted that only one pipeline stage has been configured so far, as is evident from the information provided. Refer to the following *Figure 3.8*:

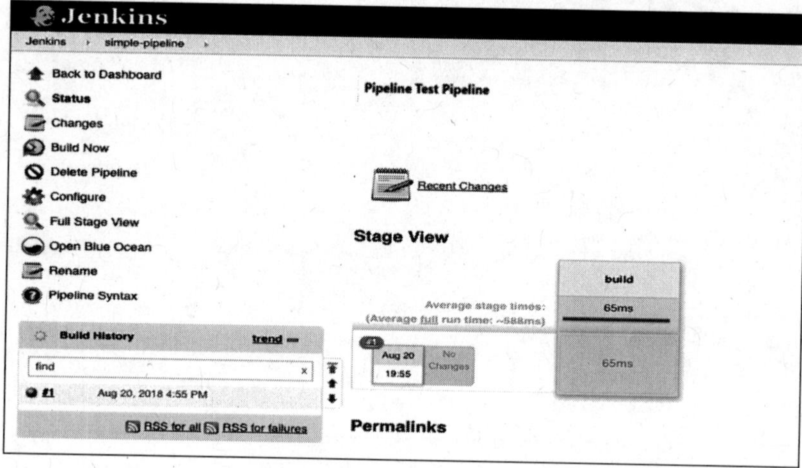

Figure 3.8: Pipeline Stage view

To confirm that the pipeline has run successfully, examine the console output of the build process. Refer to the following *Figure 3.9*:

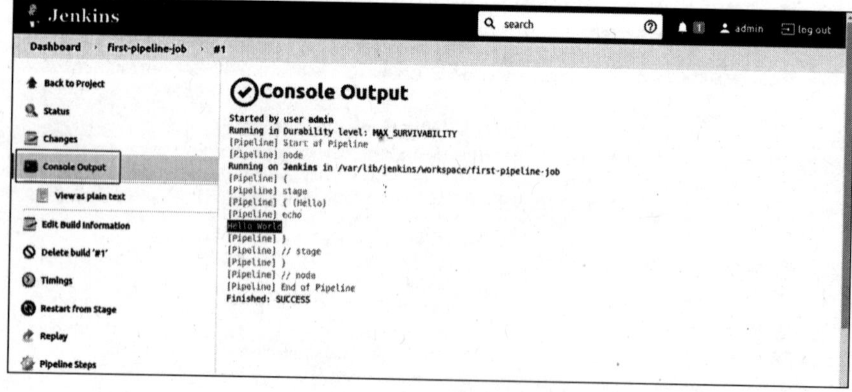

Figure 3.9: Console output

5. **Expanding the pipeline definition:** We can expand the pipeline by adding more stages to the pipeline. To accomplish this, select the **Configure** option and modify the pipeline definition as shown in the following code block:

```
pipeline {
    agent any
```

```
stages {
      stage ('Stage #1') {
    steps {
        echo  'Hello world'
        sleep 10
        echo  'This is the First Stage'
    }
}
stage ('Stage #2') {
    steps {
        echo 'This is the Second stage'
        }
    }
stage ('Stage #3') {
    steps {
        echo 'This is the Third Stage'
        }
    }
```

Save changes and click **Build Now** to execute the pipeline. After successful execution, view each new stage in **Stage View**. Refer to the following *Figure 3.10*:

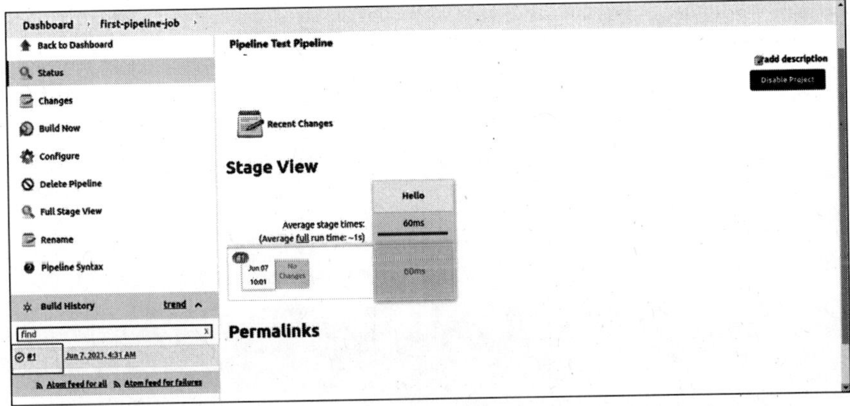

Figure 3.10: Pipeline stage view

The following console logs in *Figure 3.11* verify that the code was executed as expected:

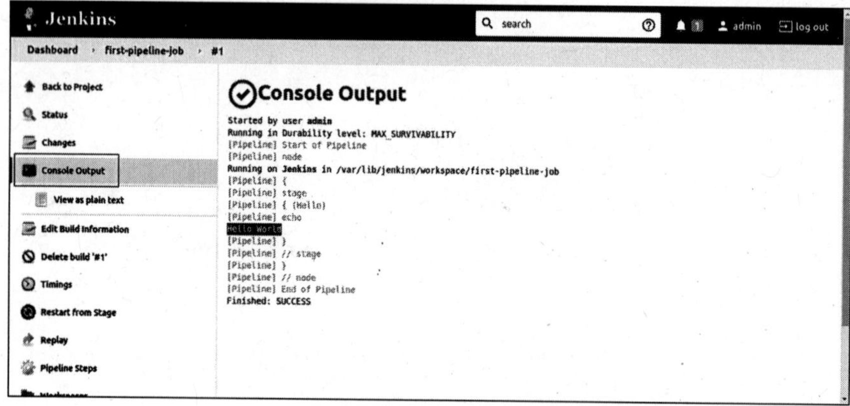

Figure 3.11: Console output

6. **Visualizing the pipeline:** For better visualization of pipeline stages, we can use the **Pipeline Timeline** plugin. After installing the plugin, navigate to the build stage and select **Build Timeline**. Refer to the following *Figure 3.12*:

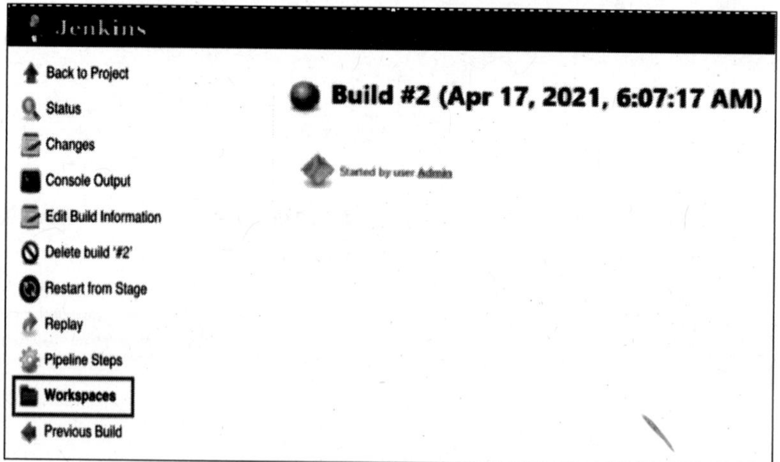

Figure 3.12: Build timeline

Click on that option, and you will be presented with a timeline of the pipeline events, as shown in the following *Figure 3.13*:

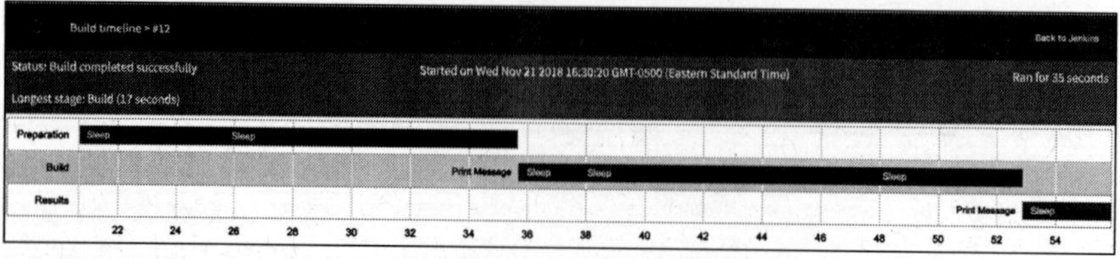

Figure 3.13: Timeline of pipeline events

After successfully configuring a CI/CD pipeline in Jenkins, the next step is to expand it by integrating external code repositories, test frameworks, and deployment strategies.

CI/CD pipelines minimize manual work

Setting up a well-designed pipeline will make the delivery team work faster and with fewer mistakes. It reduces manual tasks and improves the overall quality of the product. This leads to a quicker and more flexible development cycle, benefiting end-users, developers, and the entire business.

A well-designed and executed continuous pipeline can significantly enhance productivity, quality, and collaboration, leading to more efficient and successful outcomes for the organization or project. Regularly refining and updating the pipeline ensures its continued success in an ever-changing environment.

In the following chapters, we will explore the tools and technologies associated with continuous delivery, delve into best practices for successful implementation, and address common challenges and considerations encountered along the way.

Automation testing strategies

Automated testing is at the heart of successful CI/CD pipelines. We will explore various testing methodologies and strategies that organizations can use to achieve comprehensive test coverage and ensure the quality and reliability of software applications as they move through the CI/CD process.

Understanding automation testing

Automated testing utilizes tools and scripts to execute, compare, and report test results, consistently detecting defects and validating code changes.

Types of automation testing

The types of automation testing are as follows:

- **Unit testing:** Unit tests focus on verifying the correctness of individual code units, such as functions or methods. These tests are rapid and isolate specific sections of code for validation.

- **Integration testing:** Integration tests assess the interactions between different components or modules within an application. They ensure that integrated parts function correctly together.
- **Functional testing:** Functional tests validate that the application's features and functionalities work as expected. These tests emulate user interactions and assess the software's behavior.
- **End-to-End testing: End-to-End** (**E2E**) tests simulate complete user scenarios to validate the application workflow. They mimic fundamental user interactions and assess the software's behavior across various components.
- **Regression testing:** Regression tests ensure that new code changes do not inadvertently break existing functionalities. They help maintain the stability of the application over time.

Strategies for comprehensive test coverage

The strategies for comprehensive test coverage are as follows:

- **Test pyramid:** The test pyramid is a widely recognized strategy that advocates for more unit tests, followed by integration and E2E tests. This approach optimizes test speed and coverage.
- **Risk-based testing:** Focus testing efforts on areas of the application that are most critical or prone to errors. This strategy ensures that high-risk areas receive thorough testing.
- **Test data management:** Realistic test data can be generated and managed to simulate various scenarios and edge cases, enabling comprehensive testing of different conditions.
- **Parallel testing:** Execute tests in parallel to save time and expedite feedback. Parallel testing is beneficial for E2E tests and large test suites.
- **Continuous feedback loop:** Integrate automated tests into the CI/CD pipeline to provide rapid feedback on code changes. Automate tests to run whenever new code is committed, ensuring quick identification of issues.
- **Shift-left testing:** Begin testing early in the development process. Encourage developers to write unit tests as they code, reducing the likelihood of defects downstream.

Tooling and frameworks

Various testing tools and frameworks facilitate the implementation of automated testing strategies:

- **JUnit, NUnit, pytest:** Popular unit testing frameworks for different programming languages.
- **Cucumber, SpecFlow:** Tools for **behavior-driven development (BDD)** that enhance collaboration between technical and non-technical stakeholders.
- **Selenium, Cypress:** E2E testing frameworks for web applications.
- **Jenkins, Travis CI, CircleCI:** CI/CD platforms that enable automated test execution as part of the pipeline.

Challenges and best practices

The following are the challenges and best practices:

- **Test maintainability:** Regularly update and maintain tests to reflect changes in the application.
- **Test data management:** Ensure realistic and up-to-date test data for accurate testing.
- **Flakiness:** Address flaky tests that intermittently fail, impacting confidence in test results.
- **Continuous learning:** Stay updated on evolving testing practices, tools, and techniques.

Automated testing strategies ensure software application reliability, quality, and rapid delivery within CI/CD pipelines. Organizations can achieve comprehensive test coverage and foster a culture of continuous quality improvement by adopting a range of testing methodologies and implementing effective testing strategies. The following chapter will explore how containerization and orchestration can enhance CI/CD workflows.

Data integration in CI/CD

Integrating this data into the CI/CD pipeline ensures that applications are functionally robust and data-rich, providing users with dynamic and real-time experiences. There are different types of data sources and their integration points.

Types of data sources

The types of data sources are discussed as follows:

- **Databases:** Traditional relational databases like **MySQL** and **PostgreSQL** and modern **NoSQL** databases like **MongoDB** and **Cassandra**.
- **APIs:** External services that provide data, such as weather services, financial data providers, or social media feeds.
- **Flat files:** CSV, Excel, and other file formats that store data.
- **Streams:** Real-time data streams like **Kafka** or **AWS Kinesis**.

Integration points

The different types of integration points are as follows:

- **Direct database connections:** Connecting directly to a database to fetch or push data.
- **Middleware:** Tools like **Apache NiFi** or **Talend** that can pull data from various sources and push it to destinations.
- **Data ingestion tools:** Tools like **Logstash** or **Fluentd** specialize in collecting, transforming, and sending data.

Continuous data integration

As applications evolve, so does the data they rely on. Continuous data integration ensures that as new data becomes available, it is immediately fetched and integrated into the application, keeping its data layer updated. Tools like **Apache Kafka** facilitate real-time data integration, allowing data to be ingested as soon as it is produced or updated.

Benefits

The benefits of continuous data integration are as follows:

- **Real-time data availability:** With continuous data integration, applications can display the most recent data, enhancing user experience. For example, a stock market app shows real-time stock prices.
- **Improved data quality:** Regularly integrating and validating data can highlight inconsistencies or errors, ensuring that applications always have access to high-quality data.

- **Faster feedback loops:** Immediate data availability can speed testing and debugging. If there is an issue with the data, it is detected and rectified promptly, ensuring that the final product is both functionally and data-wise robust.

Data validation and testing

In the realm of software development, data is as crucial as code. Incorrect or corrupted data can lead to faulty outputs, even if the code is perfect. Thus, ensuring that the data integrated into applications is accurate and reliable is essential. Data validation acts as a gatekeeper, ensuring that only data that meets predefined standards and criteria enters the system.

Type of data tests

The different type of data tests are explained as follows:

- **Unit tests:** These tests focus on individual pieces of data or small datasets. For example, checking if a particular value falls within an expected range or if a string matches a specific pattern. Tools like *pytest* for Python can be used for data unit testing.
- **Integration tests:** These tests ensure that data flows seamlessly between different systems or components. For example, verifying that data fetched from an API integrates well with a database. Tools like *Postman* can test data flow between APIs and databases.
- **End-to-end tests:** A comprehensive test that validates the entire data pipeline, from the initial data source to the final destination, ensuring that data transformation, processing, and integration happen without issues. Tools like *Databand* can help in end-to-end data pipeline testing.

Data quality checks

Below are the data quality checks which helps in governance,

- **Accuracy:** Ensuring that the data in the system reflects its actual value. For example, a product's price should match its actual cost.
- **Consistency:** Data should be uniform across the system. For example, date formats should be consistent throughout.

- **Completeness:** All essential data should be included. If a user profile requires an email, it should be present.
- **Reliability:** Data should be sourced from trustworthy sources and available consistently.
- **Timeliness:** Data should be current. For example, a weather app should display today's forecast, not last week's.

Automated data testing

Manual data validation can be time-consuming and prone to errors. Automated data testing tools can validate vast amounts of data quickly and efficiently. Let us take a look at a few automated data testing tools:

- **Great Expectations:** A Python-based tool that lets you express expectations about your data as simple, declarative assertions.
- **data build tool (dbt):** You can write, document, and execute SQL-based tests on your data. It is beneficial for testing transformations and ensuring the transformed data is correct.

Integrating these tools into the CI/CD pipeline ensures that data validation occurs automatically, catching issues early in the development process.

Data deployment strategies

Data deployment is a critical aspect of the software release process, especially in applications where data drives functionality. Unlike code, which is stateless, data has a state, making its deployment a unique challenge. Effective data deployment strategies ensure that data changes are synchronized with code deployments, ensuring seamless application functionality and minimizing disruptions.

Let us discuss different deployment strategies and advantages of each.

Blue-green deployments

Concept: This strategy involves having two separate environments-the **blue environment**, which runs the current data version, and the **green environment**, which hosts the new version.

Process:

- Initially, all user traffic is directed to the blue environment.

- Data changes are deployed to the green environment and thoroughly tested.
- Once validated, traffic is gradually shifted from blue to green, making the green environment the new production environment.

Advantages:

- Minimizes downtime as the switch between environments is almost instantaneous.
- If issues arise in the green environment, traffic can quickly revert to the blue environment.

Feature toggles

Concept: This strategy allows developers to release new data features to a limited subset of users, acting as a controlled testing environment.

Process:

- New data features are hidden behind toggles or flags.
- These features can be turned on for specific users, user groups, or a percentage of users.
- Feedback from these users can guide further development or full-scale release.

Advantages:

- Enables testing new data features in a real-world environment without a full-scale release.
- Reduces risk by limiting exposure to a subset of users.

Rolling deployments

Concept: Instead of deploying data changes to all users simultaneously, changes are rolled out incrementally.

Process:

- Old data versions are gradually replaced with new versions.
- This can be done user-by-user, server-by-server, or region-by-region.

Advantages:

- During the deployment process, it is important to guarantee that the application always stays accessible to users.

- If issues arise, they affect a smaller subset of users, making them easier to manage and rectify.

Data rollback mechanisms

Even with rigorous testing and validation, data issues can still emerge post-deployment. These issues can range from minor inconsistencies to significant data corruption. Having robust rollback mechanisms in place is not just a safety net; it is a necessity. These mechanisms ensure the system can be quickly restored to stability when things go away, preserving data integrity and minimizing disruptions.

Let us discuss different data rollback mechanisms and their advantages.

Backup and restore

Concept: This is the most straightforward rollback mechanism. Regular backups of data are taken and stored securely. In the event of a data issue, the system can be restored using the latest backup.

Process:

- Scheduled backups are taken regularly, ensuring that the most recent data is always available for restoration.
- Tools like **pg_dump** for PostgreSQL or **mysqldump** for MySQL can be used to create these backups.

Advantages:

- Provides a safety net against data loss.
- Allows for quick restoration of the system to a known good state.

Data versioning

Concept: Just as code is versioned to track changes over time, data can also be versioned. This allows developers to revert to previous data states if an issue arises.

Process:

- Tools like **Data Version Control** (**DVC**) track changes in data over time.
- Each change or update to the data creates a new version, allowing developers to switch between versions as needed.

Advantages:

- Provides a historical record of data changes.
- Enables swift reversion to a previous data state, ensuring data integrity.

Automated rollback

Concept: In some advanced setups, automated scripts and tools detect data issues and initiate a rollback without manual intervention.

Process:

- Monitoring tools continuously check the health and integrity of the data.
- If an anomaly or issue is detected, predefined scripts are triggered to revert the data to its previous state.

Advantages:

- Minimizes downtime by swiftly addressing data issues.
- This helps to minimize the requirement for manual intervention, which results in a quicker recovery time.

Containerization and orchestration

In the realm of CI/CD, containerization and orchestration have emerged as pivotal technologies that revolutionize the deployment and management of software applications. In this section, we will delve into the role of container technologies like Docker and orchestration tools like Kubernetes, exploring how they enhance the efficiency, scalability, and reliability of CI/CD pipelines.

Understanding containerization

Containerization is a lightweight virtualization technique that encapsulates an application and its dependencies into isolated environments called **containers**. Containers provide consistency across different environments, from development to production, ensuring that applications behave uniformly regardless of the underlying infrastructure.

Introducing Docker

Docker is the preeminent platform for containerization. Developers can create portable containers for applications and dependencies.

The advantages of Docker include:

- **Isolation:** Containers offer strong isolation, preventing conflicts between applications and dependencies.
- **Portability:** Docker containers can run seamlessly on various platforms, from local development machines to cloud environments.
- **Efficiency:** Containers share the host OS kernel, resulting in smaller footprints and faster startup times.
- **Consistency:** Docker ensures consistency between development, testing, and production environments, minimizing the it works on my machine problem.

Orchestration with Kubernetes

As applications scale and become more complex, manual management of containers becomes impractical. This is where orchestration tools like Kubernetes come into play. Kubernetes automates containerized applications' deployment, scaling, and management, allowing teams to manage large, distributed systems efficiently.

The key features of Kubernetes include:

- **Automatic scaling:** Kubernetes dynamically adjusts the number of container instances based on demand, ensuring optimal resource utilization.
- **Load balancing:** Kubernetes distributes incoming traffic across containers to prevent overloading any single instance.
- **Self-healing:** If a container or node fails, Kubernetes automatically reschedules and replaces the failed components.
- **Configuration management:** Kubernetes enables declarative configuration, allowing you to define the desired state of your application and letting Kubernetes handle the execution details.

Containerization and CI/CD are highly complementary. By containerizing applications, teams can ensure consistent environments for testing and production. CI/CD pipelines can build, test, and deploy these containers across various stages, streamlining the delivery process. Automated testing within containers further enhances the reliability of the application.

Challenges and best practices

Following are the challenges for containerized environments:

- **Security:** Implement container security best practices, such as regularly updating base images, scanning for vulnerabilities, and using network policies.
- **Resource management:** Effectively allocate resources to containers to ensure optimal performance and prevent contention.
- **Data persistence:** Address data persistence challenges by employing strategies like external storage volumes or stateful sets in Kubernetes.

Version control and source management

Version control and source management form the bedrock of modern software development practices, and their integration within CI/CD pipelines is crucial for achieving efficient and collaborative workflows. This chapter will explore the significance of version control systems, focusing on Git and its integration into CI/CD pipelines.

Understanding version control and source management

Version control systems (**VCS**) track file changes over time, enabling multiple developers to collaborate on a codebase while maintaining a history of revisions. VCS is a foundational element for ensuring code quality, collaboration, and the ability to revert changes if needed.

Introducing Git

Git, a distributed version control system, has become synonymous with modern software development. Its decentralized architecture empowers developers to work offline, make local commits, and collaborate effortlessly with team members.

The key benefits of Git include:

- **Branching and merging:** Git allows developers to create branches for feature development, bug fixes, or experiments. Merging these branches into the main codebase promotes parallel development and organized collaboration.
- **History tracking:** Git maintains a comprehensive history of commits, making it easy to trace changes, identify contributors, and understand the evolution of the codebase.
- **Collaboration:** Git fosters collaboration by enabling seamless code-sharing between team members and facilitating efficient code reviews.

Integration within CI/CD pipelines

Incorporating version control within CI/CD pipelines provides a foundation for automation and reproducibility.

The key integration points include:

- **Versioned builds:** Using version control, CI/CD pipelines trigger builds based on specific commits or branches, ensuring consistent and reproducible artifacts.
- **Automated testing:** CI/CD pipelines can execute automated tests against specific code versions, catching bugs early in the development cycle.
- **Continuous Deployment:** Integrating version control enables CI/CD pipelines to deploy tested and approved code changes to production environments seamlessly.
- **Release management:** Version control systems aid in managing releases tagging specific commits to mark stable points in the codebase.

Git workflow strategies

Various Git workflows can optimize collaboration within development teams:

- **Feature branch workflow:** Developers create feature branches for specific features or tasks, ensuring parallel development and more accessible code review.

- **Gitflow workflow:** It incorporates branch conventions like feature, develop, release, and hotfix branches, providing a structured approach to development, testing, and release.
- **Trunk-based development:** Developers frequently integrate changes into the main branch, reducing the risk of merge conflicts and promoting continuous integration.

Challenges and best practices

Following are the challenges and best practices for Git workflows:

- **Code review:** Incorporate code review practices to maintain code quality and catch potential issues before they enter the CI/CD pipeline.
- **Version tagging:** Use version tags to label and track stable releases, ensuring clarity and traceability.
- **Branch cleanup:** Regularly clean up unused branches to keep the repository organized and reduce clutter.

Infrastructure as Code

Infrastructure as Code (**IaC**) is another fundamental DevOps practice that significantly augments testing efficiency. In the conventional approach, configuring and handling testing setups have entailed considerable time investment and susceptibility to errors. IaC empowers organizations to define and administer infrastructure configurations through code, ensuring uniform and reproducible environments. Testing teams can swiftly establish and replicate testing environments by automating infrastructure provisioning, expediting parallel test execution and minimizing reliance on manual actions. IaC further champions version control for infrastructure, simplifying rollbacks and eradicating issues tied to configuration deviations. This practice heightens testing efficiency by furnishing dependable and instantly accessible testing environments, engendering speedier feedback loops, and bolstering synergy between development and testing units.

IaC has emerged as a transformative approach to provisioning, configuring, and managing infrastructure in modern software development. This chapter will explore the principles of IaC and dive into how tools like *Terraform* and *Ansible* enable the seamless automation of infrastructure provisioning and management, enhancing the efficiency and reliability of CI/CD pipelines.

Understanding Infrastructure as Code

IaC treats infrastructure components as code artifacts, applying software engineering principles to infrastructure provisioning and management. Instead of manually configuring servers, networks, and other resources, IaC employs scripts and declarative configurations to automate these processes. The core tenets of IaC include:

- **Automation:** IaC automates the provisioning and management of infrastructure, ensuring consistency, reproducibility, and eliminating manual errors.
- **Version control:** IaC artifacts are treated like code and stored in version control systems, enabling traceability, collaboration, and control changes.
- **Reproducibility:** With IaC, infrastructure can be recreated in any environment, ensuring consistent deployments across development, testing, and production stages.
- **Consistency:** Docker ensures consistency between development, testing, and production environments, minimizing the it works on my machine problem.

Introducing Terraform

Terraform is a leading IaC tool that enables developers to declare infrastructure configurations using a domain-specific language (HCL). Some critical features of Terraform include:

- **Declarative syntax:** Terraform's approach allows developers to define the desired infrastructure state without specifying detailed procedural steps.
- **Plan and apply:** Terraform's plan and apply workflow displays the changes that will occur before applying them, providing transparency and reducing risk.
- **Provider ecosystem:** Terraform supports numerous cloud providers and services, enabling the management of diverse infrastructure components from a single codebase.

Introducing Ansible

Ansible, another popular IaC tool, takes a different approach by utilizing playbooks to define configurations. Some critical features of Ansible include:

- **Agentless architecture:** Ansible operates without requiring agents on managed nodes, making it lightweight and easy to deploy.
- **Idempotent execution:** Ansible playbooks are idempotent, meaning they can be run multiple times without changing the outcome, ensuring consistency.
- **Extensive module library:** Ansible offers a vast collection of pre-built modules to manage various infrastructure components and services.

Integration with CI/CD pipelines

Integrating IaC tools like Terraform and Ansible within CI/CD pipelines offers numerous benefits:

- **Automated infrastructure deployment:** CI/CD pipelines can automatically provision and configure infrastructure based on code changes, enabling streamlined application deployments.
- **Infrastructure validation:** IaC enables automated validation of infrastructure changes before they are applied, reducing errors and enhancing quality.

Challenges and best practices

Incorporating version control within CI/CD pipelines provides a foundation for automation and reproducibility. The key integration points include:

- **Code review:** Treat infrastructure code like application code, subjecting it to code review practices to maintain quality and security.
- **Modularity:** Organize infrastructure code into reusable modules to facilitate consistency and reduce duplication.
- **State management:** Understand and manage the state of infrastructure resources to ensure accurate tracking of changes.

Conclusion

In this chapter, we embarked on a comprehensive journey through the multifaceted world of continuous integration, continuous delivery, and the increasingly vital realm of data CI/CD. With the convergence of intricate processes and tools, we have demystified how modern software development teams can construct a resilient CI/CD pipeline that ensures seamless code integration and timely delivery of accurate data. We delved into the foundational elements, from the preliminary stages of code integration to the advanced facets of data deployment strategies. We have explored tools like Jenkins, discussed the merits of automation testing, and underscored the importance of data validation and orchestration. The insights gleaned from this chapter equip teams to reduce manual interventions, minimize errors, and streamline their development processes. By embracing the methodologies and strategies shared, development teams are positioned to harness the power of a robust CI/CD pipeline, ensuring that applications are consistently updated, accurate, and efficient.

In the next chapter, we will discuss critical aspects of continuous delivery for both software and data. We will explore topics such as real-time monitoring, observability practices, robust security measures, and strategic release management. By mastering the content of this next chapter, you will be well-equipped to navigate the complexities of modern CD. You will learn how to ensure not only the seamless deployment of software but also safeguard its integrity, optimize performance, and comply with industry standards.

CHAPTER 4
Ensuring Effective CD

Introduction

In this chapter, we will master the art of **continuous delivery** (**CD**), a pivotal aspect of modern software and data development. CD goes beyond code deployment; it encompasses a holistic approach to ensure software integrity, performance, and compliance. Throughout this chapter, we will explore key strategies and practices that enable the smooth deployment of software and uphold its quality and reliability.

Structure

The chapter covers the following topics:

- Monitoring and observability
- Security checks and compliance in CD pipelines
- Release management strategies
- Enhanced user experience in CD

Objectives

By the end of this chapter, readers will have a comprehensive understanding of CD principles and practices, which will equip them with the necessary knowledge to implement and optimize CD pipelines. The chapter will delve into crucial aspects such as monitoring, observability, security, compliance, release management strategies, application performance, and scalability. This approach will ensure software smooth and reliable deployment in modern development environments.

Monitoring and observability

CD relies heavily on real-time monitoring and observability to ensure the smooth flow of software and data through the pipeline.

Real-time monitoring and observability for CD

Implementing real-time monitoring and observability is a foundational practice in the CD. This comprehensive approach involves strategically utilizing monitoring and observability tools to seamlessly collect, store, and analyze data from diverse components within the software and data pipeline. The subsequent elucidation breaks down the critical facets of this process:

- **Monitoring and observability tools:** Organizations typically employ various monitoring and observability tools and platforms to implement real-time monitoring. These tools are designed to collect, store, and analyze data generated by various components of the software and data pipeline. A few examples of monitoring tools include *Prometheus*, for collecting and querying metrics, and *New Relic*, which offers comprehension monitoring and analytical solutions.
- **Data collection:** Real-time monitoring involves continuously collecting data from different parts of the CD pipeline. This data can include metrics related to application performance, infrastructure health, error rates, response times, and data quality.
- **Custom metrics and alerts:** Organizations often create custom metrics tailored to their specific CD process. These metrics can be based on **Key Performance Indicators** (**KPIs**) relevant to the application or data pipeline. Automated alerting systems are configured to trigger notifications when predefined thresholds are breached, ensuring that teams are promptly informed of any issues.

- **Logs and traces:** In addition to metrics, logs and traces are vital sources of information for monitoring and observability. Logs capture detailed records of events and activities within the CD pipeline, while traces provide insights into the path taken by requests and data flows across microservices and components.
- **Visualization:** Data visualization is critical to real-time monitoring. Dashboards and graphical representations of metrics and logs enable teams to gain a quick and clear understanding of the system's health. Visualization tools like *Grafana, Kibana,* or custom dashboards provide real-time insights into the CD process. Grafana allows visualization and analysis from various sources, and Kibana is helpful in logging and event data visualization.

Utilizing monitoring data for proactive issue resolution

The data collected through real-time monitoring is pivotal in proactively addressing issues within the CD pipeline. One of its primary benefits lies in detecting anomalies, performance degradation, or deviations from expected behavior early. This early detection is paramount as it allows teams to minimize the impact of potential problems and prevent issues from escalating. Automated alerting systems complement this by notifying relevant teams or individuals when predefined conditions are met or exceeded. These alerts can be fine-tuned to focus on specific metrics or events, such as high error rates, slow response times, or spikes in resource utilization.

Proactivity is a cornerstone of effective issue resolution. With real-time data and alerts at their disposal, teams can investigate and address issues before they have a chance to worsen. Engineers and DevOps teams are empowered to delve into the root causes of problems, identify bottlenecks, and take corrective actions promptly. Moreover, monitoring data contributes to continuous improvement by providing insights into historical data and patterns. This approach empowers teams to optimize the CD pipeline, adjust infrastructure, and enhance performance with data-driven decisions.

Observing data workflows for quality and consistency

In the data-centric CD, observing data workflows is central to maintaining data quality and consistency. The observability practices adopted in this context are essential for safeguarding the integrity of data:

- Data validation processes are closely monitored within the CD pipeline. These checks encompass data accuracy, completeness, and conformity to predefined standards. The continuous monitoring of data quality metrics, including completeness, accuracy, and timeliness, ensures that data adheres to established quality standards. Alerts are triggered whenever deviations from these standards occur, prompting a review and remediation process.
- Tracking data movement from source to destination is another vital aspect of observability. Data lineage provides transparency into how data moves through the pipeline and any transformations or enrichments it undergoes along the way. This visibility is instrumental in ensuring that data is transferred accurately and efficiently.
- Data consistency checks are also implemented to ensure uniformity across different stages of the CD pipeline. Discrepancies can be identified and addressed by comparing data in staging and production environments. Additionally, observability practices cater to auditing needs and ensure compliance with data governance standards and regulations. Organizations can maintain comprehensive audit trails to track data changes and access, ensuring transparency and accountability.

The implementation of real-time monitoring and observability in CD processes holds immense value. It enables teams to identify issues early, proactively address them, and uphold the quality and consistency of data workflows. These practices collectively contribute to the overall reliability and efficiency of the CD pipeline, enhancing the integrity and performance of software and data throughout their journey from development to production.

Security checks and compliance in CD pipelines

Integrating security checks and compliance measures is a foundational aspect of a robust CD pipeline. Within this framework, various practices and procedures work in tandem to fortify the security posture:

- **Automated security scans:** This essential facet involves seamlessly integrating automated security scans, encompassing **static application security testing** (**SAST**) and **dynamic application security testing** (**DAST**). These scans play a pivotal role in assessing vulnerabilities within code and applications, including potential security threats and configuration weaknesses. The automated nature of these scans ensures that security assessments are a standard part of the CD pipeline, contributing to early threat detection.
- **Dependency scanning:** Continuous monitoring of dependencies, libraries, and third-party components is critical to the CD pipeline's security arsenal. Automated tools are leveraged to identify vulnerabilities within these components. Should any vulnerabilities be detected, automated alerts are triggered, ensuring that potential security risks are swiftly addressed.
- **Code reviews and peer inspections:** Secure code reviews and peer inspections constitute a critical layer of defense against security issues. These practices involve in-depth code examinations by both automated tools and human reviewers. By enforcing code quality standards and best practices, this approach detects vulnerabilities early in the development process and encourages secure coding habits among the development team.
- **Compliance checks:** The CD pipeline is fortified with compliance checks designed to ensure that deployments align with industry-specific regulations and internal security policies. These checks cover a range of compliance requirements, including data handling, privacy, and adherence to security standards. By automating these checks, organizations can maintain a proactive stance in adhering to their compliance obligations. For example, compliance checks are required in payment systems and data security systems in financial industries, **Health Insurance Portability and Accountability Act** (**HIPPA**) and associated rules in the healthcare industry, and so on.
- **Secret management:** Secure secret management practices are incorporated to safeguard sensitive credentials, API keys, and encryption keys. These vital components of security are stored, accessed, and rotated with utmost care and security in mind. Integration with essential management services further reinforces the safeguarding of sensitive data.

Security and compliance for code and data

In the context of the CD pipeline, security and compliance extend their protective reach to encompass both code and data:

- **Secure data handling:** Security measures extend to data, encompassing practices such as encryption at rest and in transit. Access control mechanisms are deployed to curtail unauthorized access to sensitive data, upholding data privacy and ensuring compliance with data protection regulations.
- **Data quality checks:** Data quality checks are integrated into the pipeline to validate data accuracy, completeness, and integrity. Any deviations from predefined quality standards promptly trigger alerts, ensuring data integrity is maintained throughout its journey.
- **Secure code practices:** Emphasis is placed on secure coding practices that serve as a proactive defense against common vulnerabilities, including but not limited to SQL injection, **cross-site scripting** (**XSS**), and authentication flaws. Code undergoes rigorous reviews to identify and mitigate security vulnerabilities, while automated scans are employed to flag potential issues.
- **Compliance auditing:** Robust auditing mechanisms are set in motion to track and document changes to code and data meticulously. These audit trails provide comprehensive visibility into who accessed, modified, or deleted data, facilitating compliance with audit requirements and bolstering the security and compliance posture of the CD pipeline.

Security and integrity during deployment

In CD, rigorous security gates, secure deployment environments, change control, rollback mechanisms, and continuous monitoring collectively fortify the CD pipeline, ensuring code and data integrity, compliance, and resilience against security threats. Following practices mitigate risks, safeguard against data breaches, and establish a robust foundation for a trustworthy CD process:

- **Security gates:** Security gates are established within the CD pipeline to assess code and data security posture before progressing to the next stage. Any security vulnerabilities or compliance violations block deployments until issues are resolved.

- **Secure deployment environments:** The deployment environment is secured, with access controls, network segmentation, and security groups to ensure that sensitive data is protected and prevent unauthorized access.
- **Change control and approval:** Change management processes are implemented to control and approve deployments to production environments. Changes undergo rigorous security assessments and compliance checks before being allowed to proceed.
- **Rollback mechanisms:** Robust rollback mechanisms are in place to revert to a stable state in case of unexpected security incidents or issues post-deployment. These mechanisms minimize downtime and service disruptions.
- **Continuous monitoring:** Post-deployment, continuous monitoring, and auditing of the production environment ensure ongoing security and compliance. Any deviations from security baselines or compliance standards trigger alerts for immediate action.

Continuous security and compliance in CD pipelines are crucial for safeguarding code and data. Integrating security checks, enforcing compliance measures, and maintaining security practices during deployment ensure the overall security, integrity, and compliance of software and data throughout the CD process. These practices help mitigate security risks and protect against data breaches, contributing to a robust and trustworthy CD pipeline.

Release management strategies

Effective release management is pivotal for the success of CD practices, and advanced strategies can significantly enhance this process:

- Release orchestration involves meticulous planning and coordination of every aspect of a release. Advanced release management tools enable the definition of release pipelines, specifying the precise order in which components or microservices are deployed. This meticulous planning ensures that releases unfold seamlessly, minimizing disruptions to the end-users.
- A seamless integration of release management with the **continuous integration** (CI) process is a game-changer. When

code changes successfully pass CI tests, they can trigger the release process automatically. This streamlined approach accelerates code movement from the development phase to production, reducing the need for manual interventions.

- The implementation of incremental releases entails deploying manageable changes to production regularly. This approach mitigates the risks associated with significant, infrequent releases and facilitates faster user feedback, promoting a more agile development cycle.
- Creating deployment blueprints or templates that define the required infrastructure and configuration for each environment (for example, development, staging, production) is a best practice. These blueprints ensure consistency across environments and minimize the potential for configuration errors during deployments.
- Rolling deployments are employed to minimize downtime and reduce user impact. Advanced strategies involve deploying new versions to a subset of servers simultaneously, with each subset undergoing verification for stability before the rollout continues. This approach effectively isolates and resolves any issues that may arise.

Complex releases across different environments

Within CD pipelines, coordinating complex releases across diverse environments presents a challenge that demands advanced coordination strategies:

- **Environment synchronization:** Ensuring synchronization between development, staging, and production environments is crucial. Automated scripts and **Infrastructure as Code (IaC)** tools are pivotal in maintaining consistent configurations and data across environments, minimizing surprises during deployment. Ansible and Terraform are examples of tools for configuration management and infrastructure provisioning respectively. These tools are widely used by organizations to automate environment synchronization.
- **Release pipelines:** Defining separate release pipelines tailored to different environments is essential. Each pipeline outlines the steps to deploy the application or data to its respective environment. These individualized release pipelines offer granular control and traceability.

- **Environment isolation:** Implementing environment isolation is a crucial strategy to prevent changes in one environment from affecting others. This isolation may involve network segmentation, stringent access controls, and the separation of infrastructure resources to maintain the integrity of each environment.
- **Deployment approval workflow:** Establishing a rigorous approval workflow for promoting changes from one environment to another ensures that changes undergo thorough review and testing before reaching the production stage.
- **Rollback plans:** Developing comprehensive rollback plans specific to each environment is imperative. In the event of issues during deployment, well-defined rollback procedures serve as a safety net, allowing for a quick return to a stable state.

Feature toggles and rollbacks for precise control

Feature toggles, also known as **feature flags** and rollbacks, are potent techniques that provide precise control during CD:

- Implementing feature toggles empowers the enablement or disablement of specific features within an application. This approach enables gradual feature releases, testing with a select subset of users, and feedback collection before full-scale activation. Feature toggles offer meticulous control over feature status.
- Combining feature toggles with **A/B testing** enables the comparison of different feature versions in a real-world setting. This approach facilitates data-driven decisions about which version offers the best user experience.
- Canary releases entail deploying new application versions to a small, carefully selected subset of users or servers known as the **canary group** before a broader rollout. Monitoring the canary group allows for the prompt identification and resolution of issues, reducing risks associated with deploying untested changes.
- Thoughtful planning and documentation of rollback procedures for each release are essential. In the event of critical issues, rollback procedures enable a swift return to a previous, stable version of the application. Well-practiced rollback procedures minimize downtime and disruptions for users.

- Using feature flag management tools centralizes the control of feature toggles and provides monitoring capabilities for their usage. These tools offer insights into feature performance and facilitate easy toggling of features on and off.

Advanced release management strategies entail meticulous planning, orchestration, and coordination of releases. They also leverage feature toggles and rollbacks to provide precise control over feature releases and ensure minimal disruptions during deployments. These strategies enhance the reliability and flexibility of CD processes, allowing for more agile and controlled releases.

Optimizing application performance in CD optimizing your application's performance during CD involves several tactics to ensure it runs smoothly:

- **Load testing:** Load testing is a crucial starting point. Incorporate load tests into your CD pipeline to simulate real-world traffic and identify performance bottlenecks. These tests provide insights into your application's behavior under different user activity levels.
- **Performance turning:** Performance tuning should be an ongoing practice. To boost performance, continuously fine-tune your code, database queries, and system configurations. Profiling tools and performance monitoring help pinpoint areas that need improvement.
- **Caching and content delivery:** Implement caching mechanisms to temporarily store frequently accessed data or content. Additionally, **content delivery networks** (**CDNs**) can be utilized to serve static assets, reducing server load and response times.
- **Optimize your database:** Ensure your database queries, indexing, and schema design are optimized to enhance database performance. Strategies like database sharding or replication can be employed for horizontal scaling.
- **Implement resource management practices:** Practices like connection pooling optimize system resource utilization to prevent exhaustion and performance issues.

Scalability to handle workload and traffic

To ensure scalability during CD, preparing your application to handle increased workloads and traffic effectively is essential. Following are some of the approaches for scalability:

- **Auto-scaling:** It is a valuable approach. Set up auto-scaling solutions that automatically adjust resources based on traffic and demand. This ensures your application can handle surges in traffic without manual intervention.
- **Horizontal scaling:** When scaling your application, add more instances or nodes to distribute the load horizontally. Container orchestration platforms like Kubernetes can facilitate this process.
- **Microservices architecture:** Breaking your application into microservices that can scale independently allows for more granular scalability. Microservices can be deployed, scaled, and managed separately.
- **Stateless design:** Choose stateless design where possible. Stateless designs simplify scaling, as new instances can be added without concerns about shared state.
- **Database scalability:** Choose databases that support horizontal scaling, replication, and sharding. Implement strategies like database partitioning to distribute data across multiple nodes.

Ensuring high availability and performance

High availability and performance are paramount to maintaining a reliable CD pipeline in production environments. Following are some of the practices to ensure high performance in the pipelines:

- **Ensure redundancy and failover:** Run multiple instances of your application and use load balancing to distribute traffic between them. Implement failover mechanisms to automatically route traffic to healthy instances if one instance fails.
- **Develop a disaster recovery plan:** Establish a comprehensive disaster recovery plan that includes data backups, off-site storage, and recovery strategies from significant incidents. Regularly test your disaster recovery procedures.
- **Implement health checks and monitoring:** Continuously monitor the health of your production environment. Implement health checks to detect application components, infrastructure, and dependencies issues. Automated alerts should trigger an action when anomalies are detected.
- **Plan for scalability on demand:** Ensure your production environment can scale on demand to handle traffic spikes and unexpected load increases. Auto-scaling and load-balancing solutions play a crucial role here.

- **Emphasize performance monitoring and optimization:** Implement real-time performance monitoring to identify and address performance bottlenecks promptly. Monitoring should cover application response times, resource utilization, and error rates.
- **Leverage content delivery:** Utilize CDNs to distribute content closer to end-users. CDNs enhance content delivery speed and reduce latency for users in various geographic regions.

Optimizing application performance and scalability during CD involves load testing, performance tuning, resource management, and architectural choices. It is crucial to ensure your application can handle increased workload traffic and maintain high availability in production environments. These strategies provide a reliable, high-performing CD pipeline that delivers exceptional user experiences.

Enhanced user experience in CD

Enhancing **user experience** (**UX**) is pivotal during CD as it directly influences how users interact with your software. To achieve enhanced UX, following are some the best practices,

- Begin by prioritizing user-centric development. Involve UX designers and conduct user research early in the development cycle to gain insights into user needs and preferences. This understanding informs feature development and design choices.
- Use user story mapping techniques to represent user journeys and workflows visually. This facilitates team alignment on user priorities, ensuring CD efforts focus on delivering features that directly benefit users.
- Incorporate usability testing into the CD pipeline to collect direct user feedback. Usability testing provides valuable insights into user behavior and interaction.
- Ensure that user personas align with CD practices. Different user personas may have varying needs and expectations, so tailor deployment strategies and feature rollouts accordingly.

Minimizing user disruption in deployments

Minimizing user disruption during deployments is crucial for maintaining a positive user experience. To achieve this:

- Implement feature toggles (feature flags) to selectively turn new features on or off. This allows gradual feature releases to a subset of users, minimizing the impact of potential issues.

- Deploy new versions of your application to a small, carefully selected subset of users or servers (the canary group) before a full rollout. Monitor the canary group for issues and ensure a smooth transition before expanding the release.
- Utilize rolling deployments to minimize downtime and user impact. This involves deploying updates to a subset of servers at a time, with automated health checks to verify the stability of each phase before proceeding.
- Implement blue-green deployments, maintaining two identical environments (blue and green). Deploy new changes to one environment while the other serves production traffic, allowing for an immediate rollback in case of issues.
- If necessary, schedule maintenance windows during off-peak hours for deployments and updates. Communicate maintenance schedules to users in advance to manage expectations.

Collecting and incorporating user feedback

Collecting and incorporating user feedback is vital to continuous improvement in CD processes. To refine the CD practices, following are some ways to get the feedback.

- Establish clear feedback channels for users to report issues, provide suggestions, and share their experiences. These channels may include feedback forms, in-app feedback mechanisms, or user support channels.
- Regularly analyze user feedback to identify recurring issues, pain points, and areas for improvement. Categorize feedback by severity and prioritize actions accordingly.
- Create a feedback loop within development teams to ensure user feedback is acknowledged, discussed, and integrated into development plans. Regularly update users on resolved issues or implemented suggestions.
- Define user-centered metrics that align with the goals of your CD pipeline. These metrics may include user satisfaction scores (for example, *Net Promoter Score*), app performance benchmarks, and user engagement metrics.
- Use user feedback to drive iterative design and development. Implement feedback-based changes and improvements, and continuously test and refine user experiences.

In summary, enhancing user experience in CD involves:

- Prioritizing user-centric development.

- Implementing deployment strategies that minimize user disruption.
- Actively collecting and incorporating user feedback to refine CD practices.

Integrating UX considerations into the CD pipeline creates software that meets user expectations. It continually evolves to address changing needs, creating a more positive and engaging user experience.

Conclusion

In CD, prioritizing user experience is not just a best practice, it is a fundamental requirement for success. This chapter has explored strategies for enhancing user experience throughout the CD process. We emphasized the importance of embracing user-centric development. Involving UX designers, conducting user research, and mapping user journeys is vital to align CD efforts with user needs and preferences. Minimizing user disruption during deployments is essential to ensure a smooth CD process. Feature toggles, canary releases, rolling deployments, blue-green deployments, and scheduled maintenance are crucial in achieving this goal.

Continuous improvement in CD practices relies on collecting and acting upon user feedback. Establishing clear feedback channels, analyzing feedback, and creating a feedback loop within development teams are critical to continually refining CD processes.

An enhanced user experience is not just a desirable outcome but a guiding principle that should inform every stage of the CD pipeline. By prioritizing UX, minimizing disruptions during deployments, and actively engaging with user feedback, organizations can meet user expectations and exceed them. The result is a CD pipeline that delivers features quickly and ensures a positive and satisfying user experience, ultimately leading to greater user engagement and success in the modern software landscape.

In the next chapter, we will address the challenges and strategies associated with scaling **continuous integration and continuous delivery (CI/CD)** for large projects. Moreover, the chapter explores the pivotal concept of continuous improvements and feedback loops within CI/CD workflows, emphasizing the iterative nature of these practices to enhance efficiency, foster innovation, and maintain the highest software development standards. Readers can expect a comprehensive exploration of advanced CI/CD practices, providing practical guidance for optimizing deployment workflows and ensuring seamless integration across varied project scales and environments.

CHAPTER 5
Optimizing CI/CD Practices

Introduction

This chapter focuses on refining and optimizing **continuous integration and continuous delivery (CI/CD)** and data CI/CD practices. Readers will explore strategies to address the unique demands of large projects, diverse environments, and the importance of continuous improvement, specifically focusing on data integrity and quality.

Structure

The chapter covers the following topics:

- Scaling CI/CD for large projects
- CI/CD for different environments
- Continuous improvements and feedback loops

Objectives

This chapter aims to provide readers with advanced insights and strategies for refining and optimizing CI/CD and data CI/CD practices. By delving into the challenges posed by large projects and diverse environments, the chapter equips readers with the knowledge to scale CI/CD effectively. Additionally, a specific emphasis on data integrity and quality ensures that readers understand the intricacies of managing data within the CI/CD pipeline. Throughout the chapter, readers will discover actionable approaches for continuous improvement and feedback loops, fostering a culture of adaptability and efficiency in software and data development. Please refer to the following figure:

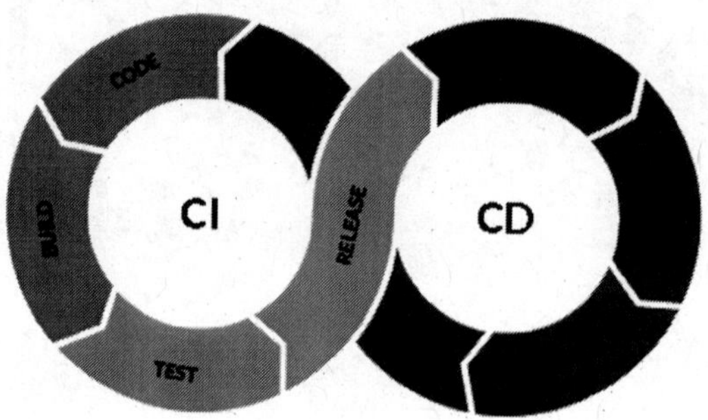

Figure 5.1: *CI/CD process*

CI/CD is a methodology to build a pipeline that integrates codes from different developers into a shared space, test the updates against requirements in testing environment, packages the validated code into a shared repository, and automatically deploy the new version. This methodology is typically practiced by agile teams following approaches such as DevOps. CI streamlines the coding and build process, whereas CD streamlines the release and deployment of the project.

Scaling CI/CD for large projects

Let us discuss the project complexity in software development. Understanding complexity is crucial because it influences how software projects are planned, executed, and managed.

Defining complexity in software development

The following points define complexity in software development:

- **Complexity dimensions:** Complexity in software development can manifest in various dimensions, each presenting its unique challenges. For example, technical complexity may arise from intricate algorithms, cutting-edge technologies, or intricate code structures. Organizational complexity can result from large development teams, distributed collaboration across multiple locations, or complicated reporting structures. Lastly, domain complexity may emerge from challenging business requirements, intricate regulatory constraints, or a rapidly evolving market landscape. Recognizing these dimensions is essential as they provide insights into which aspects of the project may be remarkably complicated.

- **Interconnectedness:** Software systems are inherently interconnected. Changes in one part of the system can have ripple effects throughout the structure. This interconnectedness adds to the complexity, as developers must consider the immediate consequences of their changes and the broader implications within the system. For example, a simple code modification may impact multiple modules, requiring extensive regression testing and validation.
- **Emergent properties:** Complexity often leads to emergent properties, system behaviors, or characteristics that cannot be easily predicted by examining individual components in isolation. For example, performance bottlenecks in a complex distributed system may emerge under certain conditions or high loads. These emergent properties require careful consideration during both the development and testing phases.

Factors contributing to increased complexity

The following factors contribute to increased complexity in software development:

- **Project size and scope:** Larger projects often increase complexity due to the sheer code volume, interactions, and dependencies. Projects with broad scopes, such as enterprise-level applications or systems, tend to have more intricate requirements that must be carefully managed and validated.
- **Dependency chains:** Dependencies among software components, libraries, and external systems can amplify complexity. Managing and updating dependencies becomes a critical aspect of project complexity management. Changes in one component may necessitate adjustments in related

dependencies, introducing challenges in maintaining compatibility.

- **Technological diversity:** Using diverse technologies, programming languages, and platforms within a project can introduce complexity. In contrast, projects that adhere to a single technology stack may have lower technical complexity, as developers can specialize in a narrower set of tools and practices.
- **Changing requirements:** Evolving or unclear requirements can add complexity. Agile development practices accommodate changing requirements more effectively by providing mechanisms to adapt to new information while managing complexity through iterative development cycles.
- **Integration challenges:** Integrating various software components, third-party services, and data sources can be a source of complexity. Challenges may arise in data integration, ensuring API compatibility, and achieving seamless system interoperability.

Impact of complexity on development and delivery

Complexity can lead to delays as developers need more time to understand, design, and implement complex features or resolve intricate issues. These delays can have cascading effects on project timelines and budgets. It can increase the likelihood of defects and make testing more challenging. Comprehensive testing strategies become indispensable in complex projects, including rigorous unit testing, integration testing, and end-to-end testing. The validation of complex system interactions requires meticulous planning and execution. Complex codebases are often more challenging to maintain and may accrue technical debt over time. Technical debt represents areas of suboptimal code or design choices made to meet immediate project goals but require future refinements. Managing technical debt through refactoring and ongoing code quality efforts is essential in complex projects. Complex projects carry higher inherent risks, including the risk of project failure, cost overruns, or suboptimal outcomes. Identifying, assessing, and mitigating these risks are essential project management responsibilities. Risk mitigation strategies may involve contingency planning, resource allocation adjustments, or project scope revisions.

By understanding the nature of complexity in software development and recognizing the contributing factors and potential impacts, development teams can better prepare for and navigate complex projects. This knowledge can inform project planning, resource allocation, and risk management strategies, ultimately leading to more successful software development and delivery.

Challenges of large projects

Here, we will explore some specific challenges often encountered in large software projects. Large projects come with a unique set of complexities that require careful consideration and management.

Identifying challenges specific to large projects

Some of the challenges related to large projects are:

- **Scope management:** Large projects frequently face the challenge of defining and managing project scope. The risk of scope creep, where the project's boundaries expand beyond the initial requirements, is particularly pronounced in larger endeavors. For example, in a large enterprise application development project, a request from stakeholder's demand enhancement of reporting functionality that was not part of the original scope. Addressing this challenge necessitates robust change management processes and disciplined scope control.
- **Communication and coordination:** Effective communication and coordination are vital in large projects involving numerous team members. Complex hierarchies and an extensive network of stakeholders can make it challenging to establish clear communication channels and ensure that information is disseminated efficiently. Implementing collaboration tools and practices becomes imperative.
- **Resource allocation:** Large projects often require a more extensive allocation of resources, including developers, testers, infrastructure, and budget. Managing resource availability and allocation becomes critical to project planning and execution. Resource shortages can lead to delays and hinder project progress.

- **Ambiguity in requirements:** In larger projects, requirements are often more complex and ambiguous. Often the business requirements are not clearly defined, leading to misunderstanding among team members. Defining and interpreting these requirements accurately is crucial. Ambiguities can lead to misunderstandings among team members and result in misaligned development efforts.
- **Integration complexity:** Large projects frequently involve numerous components, subsystems, and third-party integrations. Ensuring seamless integration and data flow across these components can be daunting. For example, the integration of a new **customer relationship management (CRM)** system with an existing one may become technical debt and defect sources if not managed meticulously.

Scalability issues in development and testing

For large projects, we see several scalability issues in different phases of the projects, such as:

- **Development scalability:** The development process needs to scale proportionally to the project's size. Strategies such as parallel development, modularization, and transparent code ownership become essential to manage development scalability. Distributed version control systems can help teams collaborate effectively. One of such examples is a large e-commerce platform where different teams work simultaneously on user interface, payment system, and inventory management.
- **Testing scalability:** Testing processes must also scale to accommodate the extensive codebase of large projects. From above e-commerce example, one might guess the vitality of testing scalability of test automation, parallel test execution, and testing environments that mirror production conditions are indispensable for efficient testing scalability. Additionally, comprehensive test coverage is essential.
- **Infrastructure scalability:** The infrastructure supporting large projects, including hardware and cloud resources, must be scalable. Ensuring the infrastructure can handle increased loads and provide the necessary computing power is vital.

Implementing scalable deployment strategies, including containerization and orchestration, can address these challenges.

Risk management in complex projects

Identifying and assessing risks is critical to managing complexity in large projects. Risks can be technical, organizational, or external. Conducting thorough risk assessments early in the project's lifecycle helps teams prepare for potential challenges. Large projects require robust risk mitigation strategies. These strategies may include contingency planning, risk transfer through insurance or contractual agreements, or adopting agile methodologies that allow teams to adapt to evolving risks. An agile approach enables incremental delivery and frequent reassessment of project priorities and risks. Effective project governance is pivotal in monitoring and mitigating risks in large projects. Governance structures provide oversight, accountability, and mechanisms for addressing project issues promptly. Governance also ensures that project objectives align with organizational goals and regulatory requirements. There is an ongoing debate about whether large projects can benefit from agile methodologies. Agile methodologies like *scrum, Kanban,* or *SAFe* which address some of these challenges. However, depending on the complexity of project a method is adapted. For example, scrum is for iterative development, Kanban is for workflow optimization, and SAFe is for scaling agile practices. Depending on the project demand, development teams can adapt Scrum, Kanban, or SAFe can be adapted to large project environments to address some of these challenges. Agile principles such as iterative development, transparency, and collaboration can help manage complexity in large projects by promoting flexibility and responsiveness to changing requirements.

By addressing these challenges head-on and implementing effective strategies for scope management, communication, scalability, risk management, and project governance, organizations can enhance their ability to execute large software projects while managing the inherent complexity successfully. Effective project management practices and agile methodologies can provide valuable tools for navigating the complexities of large-scale software development endeavors.

Codebase organization

This subsection explores strategies and best practices for organizing code within a software project to ensure maintainability, readability, and collaboration among team members.

Structuring code for maintainability

The following principles and practices stand as integral pillars for effective organization and maintainability:

- **Directory structure:** A well-organized structure is the foundation of codebase organization. It simplifies code management by providing a clear layout for code files. For example, adopting a **Model-View-Controller** (**MVC**) structure can help separate code related to data handling, user interface, and business logic. This separation enhances readability and eases navigation within the project.
- **Module and component organization:** Code can be effectively organized into modules or components, each responsible for a specific feature or functionality. This modularization promotes code reusability and facilitates maintenance. Team members can work on distinct modules independently, streamlining collaboration.
- **Naming conventions:** Consistent naming conventions are essential for codebase maintainability. They contribute to code readability and convey the purpose of each element. Guidelines for choosing meaningful and descriptive names for files, classes, functions, and variables should be established and followed diligently.
- **Code separation:** The principle of **separation of concerns** (**SoC**) advocates the separation of different aspects of an application, such as data handling, business logic, and presentation. Adhering to SoC enhances code maintainability by reducing interdependencies between components. Changes in one concern are less likely to impact others, simplifying troubleshooting and updates.

Code documentation and commenting

Clear and comprehensive documentation is invaluable in a codebase. Well-documented code simplifies onboarding for new team members, assists in understanding complex algorithms, and aids in troubleshooting. It is a crucial reference for developers, ensuring the code's intent and functionality are well-understood. Comments and annotations provide context and explanations within the code. They are beneficial for documenting complex algorithms, specifying preconditions, or clarifying non-obvious code behavior. However, comments should be used judiciously, focusing on critical areas that require clarification. Documentation tools and platforms can streamline creating and maintaining documentation. Tools like *Javadoc, Markdown-based* documentation systems allow developers to generate documentation directly from code comments. These tools ensure that documentation stays synchronized with code changes.

Version control strategies for large codebases

Following are some of the version control strategies:

- **Git workflow:** Version control systems like Git are indispensable for codebase management. Common Git workflows, such as Gitflow or feature branching, help teams manage changes in large codebases. Branching strategies provide isolation for feature development, bug fixes, and experimentation.
- **Pull requests and code review: Pull requests (PRs)** are pivotal in code collaboration and review. They facilitate peer review, conflict resolution, and merging changes into the main codebase. Effective code review ensures code quality and adherence to coding standards.
- **Branch naming conventions:** Consistent branch naming conventions are essential for clarity. Meaningful branch names provide insight into the purpose of each branch, making it easier for team members to understand the context of ongoing work.
- **Release management:** In large codebases, release management is crucial for coordinating software updates. Strategies for versioning, tagging, and release planning should be established. Automated deployment pipelines can simplify the release process, ensuring that code changes are deployed seamlessly.

Best practices and tools

In addition to the discussed practices, teams can employ various tools and extensions to further enhance code organization, documentation, and version control. These tools may include static code analyzers to enforce coding standards, documentation generators, and collaboration platforms that support code reviews and discussions.

By implementing these code organization practices, development teams can create a structured and maintainable codebase that fosters collaboration, reduces code debt, and facilitates efficient development and maintenance in large software projects. Codebase organization is a foundational aspect of project management and contributes significantly to project success.

Code review and collaboration

This subsection explores the significance of code reviews in large projects, collaborative coding practices, and code review tools and processes.

Significance of code reviews

Code reviews play a pivotal role in maintaining code quality and fostering collaboration, particularly in the context of large software projects:

- **Quality assurance:** One of the foremost roles of code reviews is ensuring code quality. By subjecting code changes to peer scrutiny, teams can identify and rectify issues such as bugs, code smells, and code standards violations before propagating to production environments. This quality assurance process becomes even more critical in large projects with extensive codebases.
- **Knowledge sharing:** Code reviews serve as invaluable platforms for knowledge sharing among team members. New developers can learn from the expertise of more experienced colleagues, gaining insights into the project's codebase and best practices. Moreover, these collaborative interactions help foster a sense of shared ownership of the codebase.
- **Consistency and standards:** Consistency across the codebase is vital for maintainability and comprehensibility. Code

reviews enforce coding standards and consistency, ensuring the code adheres to established guidelines and best practices. In large projects where numerous developers may contribute, maintaining this consistency is a significant challenge that code reviews help address.

- **Early detection of issues:** Code reviews act as a vigilant gatekeeper, identifying issues early in development. Detecting and addressing issues at this stage significantly reduces the cost and effort required for remediation. Early detection is especially crucial in large projects where the impact of issues can be more far-reaching.

Collaborative coding practices

Effective collaboration in large projects relies on various practices and approaches:

- **Pair programming:** Pair programming involves two developers working collaboratively on the same code. One developer is coding (driver) and the other one doing the review (observer). In pair programming, the combine effort of two developers working together is considered to be more effective than sum of their individual efforts. This practice promotes real-time feedback, joint problem-solving, and improved code quality. Pair programming can be a powerful approach in large projects where complex challenges often arise.
- **Code pairing:** Code pairing extends collaboration to multiple team members who work in parallel on different parts of the codebase. This approach accelerates development, leverages the strengths of various team members, and helps tackle complex tasks more efficiently.
- **Cross-functional teams:** Building cross-functional teams that bring together developers, testers, designers, and other roles is essential for fostering collaboration. Diverse perspectives and expertise contribute to well-rounded solutions and innovative problem-solving, especially in large, multifaceted projects.
- **Documentation and knowledge sharing:** Effective collaboration necessitates accessible documentation and knowledge-sharing platforms. Tools like *wikis*, documentation generators, and chat platforms enable team members to communicate, share insights, and document essential project

information. These tools are instrumental in large projects where information flow can be challenging.

Challenges in collaboration

There are some challenges and risks associated with cross-functional teams and collaborative coding practices:

- **Communication challenges:** Diverse skillset and backgrounds of different developers create differences in terminology, priorities, and perspectives to hinder effective collaboration. Conflicting personalities or working styles can also lead to tension and a reduction in productivity.
- **Conflict resolution:** The presence of individuals with varied expertise may result in conflicts regarding decision-making or the approach to solving problems. There is an assumption about bringing comparable knowledge and skills, but often significant disparities may result in hinderance in development.
- **Workload distribution:** Ensuring equitable distribution of tasks and responsibilities among team members with varied expertise can easily lead to fatigue and burnout for some team members with critical skills.

Code review tools and processes

To maintain an efficient and organized code review process within large teams, it is imperative to adhere to established procedures. Failure to do so could result in missed deadlines, increased errors, and a lack of accountability. So, the below defined processes are to be followed:

- **Code review tools:** The software industry widely uses numerous code review tools and platforms. These include *GitHub*, *GitLab*, *Bitbucket*, and *Review Board*. These tools streamline the code review process, providing structured environments for collaboration and feedback.
- **Pull requests:** Pull requests or **merge requests** (**MRs**) are central to the code review process. Developers create PRs to propose changes, and reviewers provide feedback and approval before merging the code into the main codebase. PRs offer transparency, accountability, and traceability, which are crucial in large projects.

- **Code review guidelines:** Effective code reviews require clear guidelines. Reviewers should assess code quality, functionality, security, and coding standards adherence. Constructive feedback is vital for productive reviews. Guidelines help maintain consistency and ensure that reviews are thorough and focused.
- **Automated code review:** Automated code review tools and linters complement human code reviews by identifying common issues and enforcing coding standards. These tools perform static code analysis, highlighting potential problems and ensuring adherence to coding guidelines.

Best practices and processes

In large projects, the following best practices enhance code review and collaboration:

- **Setting review timeframes:** Define clear review timeframes to ensure code changes are reviewed promptly without causing delays. Timeliness is crucial in large projects with tight development schedules.
- **Balancing thoroughness and speed:** Strike a balance between thoroughness and speed in code reviews. While comprehensive reviews are essential, the process should allow project progress. Considerations include the criticality of the code changes and the project's urgency.
- **Fostering a positive code review culture:** Cultivate a culture of respect, collaboration, and constructive feedback in code reviews. Encourage open communication and a shared commitment to code quality.

By emphasizing the importance of code reviews, promoting collaborative coding practices, and implementing practical code review tools and processes, development teams in large projects can enhance code quality, foster knowledge sharing, and streamline the development workflow. Effective collaboration and code quality are cornerstones of project success in large-scale software endeavors.

Parallelization in CI/CD

In this subsection, we will discuss the concept of parallelization in CI/CD and explore its significance, strategies, and associated benefits and challenges.

Understanding parallel CI/CD pipelines

In CI/CD optimization, parallelization emerges as a vital strategy, revolutionizing the software delivery process by maximizing resource utilization. Let us delve into the key aspects of this approach:

- **Parallelization overview:** Parallelization involves executing multiple tasks or stages concurrently in the pipeline. It is a fundamental practice to expedite software delivery by optimizing the utilization of available resources.
- **Pipeline stages:** A typical CI/CD pipeline comprises multiple stages, including code compilation, testing, artifact creation, and deployment. Parallelization allows these stages to run concurrently, significantly reducing the time required for the entire process.
- **Distributed processing:** Parallelization is synonymous with distributed processing. It entails distributing workloads across multiple machines or nodes, enabling tasks to run simultaneously. Build agents or runners play a crucial role in managing parallel processing, ensuring efficiency in the pipeline.

Parallel testing and building strategies

Embracing parallelization in testing and building processes presents many advantages for agile and efficient software development. Let us explore the key dimensions of this approach:

- **Parallel testing:** Parallelizing testing tasks, such as unit tests, integration tests, and end-to-end tests, offers several advantages. By running these tests concurrently, development teams receive faster feedback, reducing the time spent waiting for test results.
- **Parallel building:** Strategies for parallelizing the building process including code compilation, artifact packaging, and binary generation. This parallel approach accelerates the

software delivery pipeline, allowing for more frequent releases and enhanced development speed.

- **Test environment isolation:** Ensuring the isolation of test environments is paramount in parallel testing. This prevents interference between parallel test runs and maintains the integrity of test results. Techniques like containerization or virtualization are often employed to achieve environment isolation.
- **Splitting test suites:** An intelligent division of test cases into smaller, more manageable subsets is essential for large projects with extensive test suites. These subsets can be executed concurrently, reducing testing time and facilitating faster feedback loops.

Benefits and challenges of parallelization

In this section, we will explore the benefits and challenges of parallelizing CI/CD pipelines.

Benefits

Parallelizing CI/CD pipelines yields numerous benefits, including:

- **Faster feedback loops:** Developers receive rapid feedback on code changes, enabling them to address issues promptly.
- **Reduced build and test times:** Parallel execution significantly reduces the time required for building and testing code.
- **Improved resource utilization:** Efficient utilization of resources, including hardware and infrastructure.
- **Increased development speed:** Faster delivery of software and shorter release cycles.
- **Resource scalability:** Parallelization enables teams to scale resources horizontally. Additional build agents or nodes can be seamlessly added to meet increased demands, offering elasticity, especially in cloud-based CI/CD infrastructure.

Challenges

While parallelization brings substantial benefits, it also presents challenges, including:

- **Resource contention:** Managing resource contention when multiple tasks compete for the same resources.

- **Coordination of parallel tasks:** Coordinating parallel tasks to ensure they run efficiently and without conflicts.
- **Infrastructure costs:** The potential increase in infrastructure costs due to the need for more hardware resources.
- **Testing dependencies:** Managing dependencies between tests when they rely on shared resources or data. Interdependent tests may require synchronization mechanisms to prevent conflicts.
- **Parallelization tools and technologies:** Several CI/CD platforms and tools support parallelization, such as *Jenkins, Travis CI, CircleCI,* and *GitLab CI/CD*. These tools enable the configuration of parallel pipelines and provide execution environments that streamline parallel processing.

Developing teams can significantly reduce development and testing cycle times by understanding and implementing parallelization strategies in CI/CD pipelines. This results in faster software delivery, improved productivity, and enhanced collaboration between development and testing teams, ultimately contributing to the project's success.

Optimization techniques

In this subsection, we will explore optimization techniques that enhance the efficiency and effectiveness of CI/CD pipelines. These techniques encompass performance optimization, resource utilization, and cost-saving measures, along with implementing caching and artifact management.

Performance optimization in CI/CD

A strategic approach involves not only measuring key performance metrics but also implementing optimization techniques. Let us delve into the foundational elements of this optimization journey:

- **Pipeline performance metrics:** The first step in optimizing CI/CD pipelines is to measure and monitor key performance metrics. These metrics include build times, test execution times, proper logging mechanism, and deployment durations. By continuously tracking these metrics, teams can identify bottlenecks and areas that require improvement.

- **Parallelization for speed:** As discussed in the previous subsection, parallelization is crucial in optimizing pipeline performance. By distributing tasks across multiple nodes or agents, parallelization accelerates pipeline execution, leading to faster feedback and quicker software delivery.
- **Build and test optimization:** Strategies for optimizing build and test processes involve fine-tuning various aspects of the pipeline. This includes optimizing compiler settings, minimizing unnecessary steps in the build process, evaluating logs with extreme resource utilization and running only the tests relevant to the code changes.
- **Artifact minimization:** Another critical aspect of performance optimization is reducing the size of artifacts generated during the CI/CD pipeline. This can be achieved by eliminating unnecessary dependencies or resources from the final deployment package, resulting in faster artifact transfer and storage.

Resource utilization and cost savings

Optimizing resource management is crucial for efficiency and cost-effectiveness. Let us explore key strategies in this realm:

- **Elastic scaling:** Cloud-based CI/CD platforms offer elastic scaling, allowing teams to allocate resources dynamically based on demand. This flexibility not only optimizes resource utilization but also provides cost-efficient scaling options.
- **Idle resource management:** To minimize costs, teams should implement strategies for managing idle resources during periods of low demand. This may involve automatically scaling down or pausing infrastructure to avoid unnecessary expenditure.
- **Resource sharing:** Resource sharing is a cost-effective approach where multiple CI/CD pipelines share a common infrastructure. This reduces resource duplication and associated costs while ensuring efficient utilization.
- **Spot instances and preemptible VMs:** Cost-effective options like spot instances, **Amazon Web Services (AWS)**, or preemptible **virtual machines (VMs)** (Google Cloud) can be employed for build and test environments. While these options

offer significant cost savings, they come with the trade-off of potential interruptions.

- **Use of local resources:** Often a large part of development and testing could be done on local resource before moving to expensive cloud resources. Unless it is mandated to do so, a lot of experimental work, small simulations, testing, and so on. could be done without utilizing cloud resources, adding to overall cost reduction.

Implementing caching and artifact management

Optimizing artifact handling and management is instrumental. Let us cover the key practices that contribute to efficiency and reliability:

- **Caching dependencies:** Caching dependencies and build artifacts can significantly reduce build times. This involves storing frequently used dependencies and artifacts and retrieving them as needed. Caching can be implemented at the CI/CD tool level or within build scripts.
- **Artifact management tools:** Artifact management tools like *Artifactory, Nexus,* or *AWS S3* provide a structured way to store and retrieve build artifacts. These tools enable artifact versioning, access control, and efficient management of artifacts.
- **Artifacts as build outputs:** Build artifacts should be considered as part of the CI/CD pipeline's output. Consistently tracking and systematically storing artifacts ensures their accessibility for deployment and serves as a reliable reference for future use.
- **Artifact lifecycle:** Managing the lifecycle of build artifacts involves defining retention policies, archiving older artifacts, and eventually deleting those no longer needed. Balancing storage costs with compliance requirements is essential in this process.
- **Optimization planning:** Organizations must create a well-defined plan tailored to their needs and infrastructure. Optimization efforts should be iterative, with regular reviews and adjustments based on performance data and evolving requirements.

By implementing these optimization techniques, development teams can streamline their CI/CD pipelines, reduce resource waste, and improve overall efficiency. This leads to faster and more cost-effective software delivery, ultimately enhancing the organization's competitiveness and agility in the software development landscape.

Data challenges in large projects

In this subsection, we will explore the specific data-related challenges in large software projects, focusing on handling large datasets in development and testing, data synchronization challenges, and data versioning and management.

Handling large datasets in development and testing

The sheer volume of data can exert a significant influence on development and testing processes, impacting factors such as storage requirements, data transfer times, and processing speed. This challenge becomes particularly pronounced in applications dealing with big data, analytics, or multimedia content. Let us explore the key strategies for managing this data-centric challenge:

- **Volume of data:** Dealing with large datasets is a common challenge in large software projects. The sheer volume of data can impact various aspects of development and testing, including storage requirements, data transfer times, and processing speed. This challenge is particularly pronounced in big data, analytics, or multimedia content applications.
- **Data subset generation:** To address the challenge of large datasets, teams often resort to generating data subsets or synthetic data for development and testing purposes. This approach involves creating representative subsets of the dataset or crafting synthetic data that simulate real-world scenarios. By working with subsets, developers and testers can avoid the complexity of handling entire datasets, leading to more efficient and focused testing.
- **Data masking and anonymization:** Data masking and anonymization techniques are crucial in projects involving sensitive or confidential data. These practices allow teams to protect sensitive data while retaining its structure

and characteristics. Data masking involves replacing sensitive information with fictional but realistic data, while anonymization ensures that individuals' identities cannot be discerned from the data. These practices are essential for compliance with data privacy regulations like **General Data Protection Regulation** (**GDPR**) and **Health Insurance Portability and Accountability Act** (**HIPAA**).

Data synchronization challenges

Datasets from diverse sources often come with distinct schemas and update frequencies, necessitating meticulous efforts to maintain data consistency and integrity across the entire application. Let us explore the key considerations in navigating this:

- **Multiple data sources:** Large projects often involve data from various sources or databases, each with its schema and update frequency. Managing data from diverse sources can be complex, as it requires ensuring data consistency and integrity across the entire application. Synchronizing data from various sources with different formatting, while maintaining data quality is a substantial challenge.
- **Asynchronous updates:** As applications become more distributed and interconnected, data updates may occur asynchronously across different systems. This poses challenges in managing the synchronization of data changes. For example, when data is modified in one part of the application, it may need to be synchronized with other parts that rely on the updated data. Coordinating these updates while avoiding conflicts is a complex task.
- **Concurrency control:** In scenarios where multiple users or processes can update data simultaneously, concurrency control mechanisms become essential. These mechanisms ensure data integrity by preventing conflicts and inconsistencies. Optimistic locking allows multiple users to access data concurrently, and conflicts are resolved when saving changes. On the other hand, pessimistic locking involves locking data to prevent concurrent access. Both these approaches are employed to address challenges related to concurrency.

Data versioning and management

Let us explore key aspects of ensuring effective data handling and governance:

- **Data versioning:** Data versioning involves tracking changes to datasets over time. It allows teams to maintain historical records of data modifications, enabling auditing, rollback, and reproducing specific data states. Data versioning is particularly important when dealing with evolving data in large projects.
- **Data schema evolution:** Data schemas may need to evolve to accommodate changing application requirements. This evolution can involve adding, modifying, or removing fields in the data schema. Effective data versioning and management practices help organizations manage these schema changes and migrations while ensuring data consistency and integrity.
- **Data governance:** Data governance practices are crucial in addressing data challenges. It encompasses data cataloging, metadata management, and access controls. Organizations can ensure data quality, compliance, and effective data management by cataloging and documenting data assets, maintaining metadata, and enforcing access controls.
- **Data testing considerations:** Data testing is a critical aspect of data management in large projects. It involves various strategies, including data validation, integrity checks, and quality assurance processes. Data testing ensures that the data used in development and testing is accurate, consistent, and reliable.

By recognizing and addressing data challenges in large software projects through data subset generation, data masking, data versioning, and effective data governance, development teams can ensure that data remains a manageable and valuable asset in their software development lifecycle. These practices contribute to the overall success and reliability of large-scale software applications.

CI/CD for different environments

This subsection explores the different environments within a CI/CD pipeline, including development, testing, staging, and production environments. We will define these environments, outline the roles and responsibilities associated with each, and discuss environment-specific tools and configurations.

Defining environments in CI/CD

In the lifecycle of software development, distinct environments serve specific purposes. Let us explore the key stages of these environments:

- **Development environment:** The development environment is the initial stage where developers write, modify, and test code. It is often the sandbox for creating and iterating on new features and fixes. Developers work in this environment, which may include local development setups. Code changes are frequently committed and pushed to version control systems.
- **Testing environment:** In the testing environment, various types of tests are executed to assess the functionality, performance, and quality of the software. This includes unit tests, integration tests, and end-to-end tests. The testing environment should closely resemble the production environment to identify issues accurately.
- **Staging environment:** The staging environment replicates the production environment as closely as possible. It is the final checkpoint before the code is deployed to production. Here, final testing, **User Acceptance Testing** (**UAT**), and pre-production validation occur. Stakeholders, including release managers, often play a significant role in this environment.
- **Production environment:** The production environment is the operational environment where the application or service is accessible to end-users. It is the environment where the software runs at scale to serve its intended purpose. High availability, reliability, and performance are paramount in the production environment.

Roles and responsibilities in different environments

In this section, let us explore the roles and responsibilities of various environments:

- **Development environment responsibilities:** In the development environment, developers are responsible for coding, implementing new features, and fixing bugs. They also perform unit testing and ensure code quality. Collaboration via version control systems is crucial in this phase.

- **Testing environment responsibilities:** The testing environment is where **quality assurance** (**QA**) engineers and testers shine. Their responsibilities include performing tests, documenting defects, and ensuring software quality.
- **Staging environment responsibilities:** Release managers and stakeholders are actively involved in the staging environment. They oversee final validation, UAT, and approval for release. It is a phase where the readiness of the software for production is assessed comprehensively.
- **Production environment responsibilities:** In the production environment, system administrators, DevOps engineers, and production support teams take charge. Their responsibilities include managing and maintaining the production infrastructure, ensuring high availability, and responding to incidents promptly. Security and monitoring are vital aspects of their roles.

Environment-specific tools and configurations

Following are some of the environment specific tools:

- **Development environment tools:** Common tools in development environments include **integrated development environments** (**IDEs**) or code editors, local development servers, and version control systems like Git. Collaboration and code-sharing tools facilitate teamwork.
- **Testing environment tools:** Testing environments often feature test automation tools, continuous integration servers (for example, Jenkins, Travis CI), and testing frameworks tailored to the project's tech stack. Test data management tools help set up test environments effectively.
- **Staging environment tools:** For configuring and deploying applications in the staging environment, deployment orchestration tools like *Ansible* or *Kubernetes* come into play. Load balancers and monitoring tools assist in pre-production validation.

- **Production environment tools:** A robust infrastructure and configuration management tools like *Terraform* are crucial in a production environment to maintain consistency and manage **Infrastructure as Code (IaC)**. Security tools and monitoring solutions are indispensable for ongoing operations.
- **Environment consistency and parity:** Achieving consistency and parity between environments is essential to minimize discrepancies that can lead to deployment issues. IaC practices, containerization, and configuration management tools help maintain environment consistency.

By clearly defining and meticulously managing different environments within the CI/CD pipeline, organizations can ensure that their software undergoes rigorous testing, thorough validation, and reliable delivery to end-users. These practices enhance software quality and stability, ultimately leading to more successful and resilient software products.

Environment-specific challenges and considerations

In this subsection, we explore the unique challenges associated with each environment within a CI/CD pipeline, discuss strategies for maintaining consistency across environments, and delve into managing environment-specific data.

Unique challenges in each environment

Every environment has its unique challenges, following are some challenges detailed for different environments:

- **Development environment challenges:** The development environment presents distinct challenges. Developers often work with diverse local configurations, leading to compatibility and integration issues when merging code changes. Ensuring access to realistic test data for local development is also a concern. This statement raises a concern because it highlights the challenge of providing developers with access to realistic test data for local development. In software development, having relevant and representative test data is crucial for testing and validating the functionality of the application in a realistic environment. Without access to such data, developers may face difficulties in accurately simulating real-world scenarios and ensuring that their code behaves as expected in different situations. This concern underscores the importance of establishing mechanisms or processes to facilitate the availability of appropriate test data for local development, contributing to more effective and reliable software testing and development practices.

- **Testing environment challenges:** In the testing environment, coordination is critical. Different tests, including integration, unit, and end-to-end tests, must be orchestrated effectively. Managing test environments with varying configurations can be complex, and ensuring test data accurately represents production scenarios is crucial.
- **Staging environment challenges:** The staging environment mirrors production, but ensuring parity can be challenging. Discrepancies between staging and production environments can lead to unexpected issues. Maintaining data consistency and conducting thorough UAT is vital for successful staging.
- **Production environment challenges:** The production environment is the most critical, with high availability requirements. Monitoring for performance and security is paramount. Achieving zero-downtime deployments while scaling resources to meet user demand adds complexity to this environment.

Maintaining consistency across environments

For streamlined and consistent software development practices, several key principles and technologies play a pivotal role. Let us explore some of these essential elements:

- **IaC:** IaC principles are instrumental in achieving consistency. By defining and provisioning infrastructure through code, organizations ensure that the same infrastructure configurations are applied consistently across all environments. IaC tools and scripts enable repeatability and versioning.
- **Containerization:** Containerization technologies like Docker offer a solution for packaging applications and their dependencies. Containers ensure that the same application image can be deployed across all environments, from

development to production, eliminating configuration disparities.

- **Configuration management:** Configuration management tools such as *Ansible, Puppet,* and *Chef* are crucial in managing environment-specific configurations. They enforce consistency by automating the configuration of servers and services, ensuring that settings are versioned and aligned.

Managing environment-specific data

To maintain data management and environment consistency, addressing data challenges is crucial for reliable and consistent software delivery. The following points cover the key strategies and practices that organizations employ:

- **Data subsetting:** To address data challenges, organizations employ data subsetting. This practice involves creating data subsets or synthetic data for development and testing environments to mimic production scenarios. Various tools and strategies are available for generating representative data subsets.
- **Data masking:** Data masking and anonymization techniques protect sensitive data in non-production environments while preserving data realism. Proper management of data is necessary to comply with data privacy laws such as GDPR and HIPAA.
- **Database snapshots:** Database snapshots or clones replicate production data for testing and staging environments. These mechanisms ensure data remains consistent across different environments, facilitating realistic testing scenarios.
- **Environment drift mitigation:** Continuous monitoring and drift detection mechanisms are essential to identify environment inconsistencies or deviations. Automated testing and validation checks catch drift early in the CI/CD pipeline, reducing the risk of environment-related issues.
- **Real-world examples:** Real-world examples and case studies showcase how organizations have successfully tackled environment-specific challenges and maintained consistency across their CI/CD pipeline. These insights offer valuable lessons on managing environment-specific data and minimizing discrepancies, leading to more reliable and consistent software delivery.

By acknowledging and addressing the unique challenges of each environment, implementing consistency measures, and managing data effectively, organizations can ensure that their CI/CD pipeline consistently delivers software from development to production with minimal deployment risks and consistent behavior across environments.

Configuration management for code and data

In this subsection, we explore the principles of **Configuration as Code (CaC)**, managing environment configurations, data configuration and migration strategies.

Configuration as Code principles

CaC is a practice that treats infrastructure and application configurations as code artifacts. These configurations are managed and versioned like code, making them accessible through version control systems. In essence, CaC brings the benefits of code management to configurations.

Benefits of CaC

Adopting CaC principles offers numerous advantages. It improves the consistency, repeatability, and traceability of infrastructure changes. With CaC, you can automate the provisioning and configuration of infrastructure components, reducing manual errors and ensuring predictable deployments.

Tools for CaC

Popular CaC tools and platforms include Terraform, AWS CloudFormation, and Kubernetes manifests. These tools allow organizations to define, manage, and version infrastructure and application configurations in a structured and code-centric manner.

Managing environment configurations

The key aspects of environment-specific configuration management, emphasizing practices that enhance flexibility and maintain versioned configurations, are as follows:

- **Environment-specific configuration files:** Managing environment configurations involves maintaining environment-specific configuration files. These files store settings like database connection strings, API endpoints, and feature flags. Configuration management tools provide centralized configuration storage and distribution.
- **Configuration overrides:** Organizations often need to customize configurations for specific environments. Techniques like environment variables or parameterized configuration templates enable configuration overrides, ensuring flexibility while maintaining versioned configurations.
- **Versioned configuration:** Versioning configuration files alongside code is essential. This practice ensures that configuration changes are tracked and synchronized with code changes, eliminating configuration drift and providing transparency into the evolution of configurations.

Data configuration and migration strategies

The key aspects of data configuration management and related practices, emphasizing the critical role they play in maintaining data integrity and application behavior are as follows:

- **Data configuration management:** Managing data-related configurations is crucial, including database schemas, data transformation scripts, and data access policies. Changes to data configurations can significantly impact application behavior and data integrity.
- **Database migrations:** Database migration strategies involve schema migrations, data migrations, and versioning databases. Automating database schema changes through tools and practices streamlines the process and ensures that databases evolve in sync with application code.
- **Data pipeline configuration:** Data pipeline configurations, including **extract, transform, load** (**ETL**) processes, can be defined as code and managed through CaC principles. Tools like *Apache Airflow* enable the orchestration of data workflows, promoting automation and consistency.
- **Testing and validation of configurations:** The testing and validation of infrastructure and data-related configurations are

critical steps. It ensures that configurations work as intended, do not introduce issues, and are compatible with code changes.

By applying CaC principles, effectively managing environment-specific configurations, and employing data configuration and migration strategies, organizations can achieve greater consistency, automation, and reliability in their CI/CD pipelines, resulting in more efficient software delivery.

Continuous improvements and feedback loops

Continuous improvements and feedback loops are integral elements of an agile and responsive development ecosystem. Embracing a mindset of constant improvement allows teams to enhance their processes and deliver higher-quality software. The synergy between continuous improvements and feedback loops creates a dynamic environment where insights from various sources drive iterative enhancements.

Importance of feedback in CI/CD

In this subsection, we will explore the significance of feedback in CI/CD. We will discuss feedback as a cornerstone of CI/CD, real-time feedback mechanisms, and early and frequent feedback benefits.

Feedback as a cornerstone of CI/CD

Feedback in CI/CD refers to the vital information and insights gathered from various stages of the development and delivery pipeline. It encompasses all facets of software development, from code quality to user experience. In essence, feedback serves as the compass that guides the CI/CD process.

Iterative development

CI/CD is built on the principle of iterative development. Each iteration involves making incremental changes based on feedback. This iterative approach allows for constant refinement, adaptation, and course correction, all made possible by the continuous flow of feedback.

Continuous improvement

Feedback is the cornerstone of constant improvement in CI/CD. The pipelines are designed to deliver software and collect data and insights at every step. These insights drive process enhancements, code quality, and overall software delivery.

Real-time feedback mechanisms

The key components that play a pivotal role in providing instantaneous insights and promoting continuous improvement are as follows:

- **Automated testing:** Automated testing, including unit tests, integration tests, and end-to-end tests, is pivotal in providing real-time feedback. After code changes, test results are generated immediately, revealing code quality and functionality issues. This rapid feedback loop accelerates development cycles.
- **Static code analysis:** Static code analysis tools deliver real-time feedback by identifying code quality issues, security vulnerabilities, and deviations from coding standards. Developers receive instant insights, empowering them to make improvements as they code.
- **Monitoring and logging:** In production environments, monitoring and logging mechanisms offer real-time feedback on application performance, error rates, and user behavior. By proactively detecting incidents and issues, teams can respond swiftly and maintain high availability.
- **User feedback:** User feedback mechanisms, such as user surveys, feedback forms, and user analytics, provide real-time insights into user preferences and issues. This direct feedback loop informs user-centric improvements, ensuring the software meets user expectations.

Benefits of early and frequent feedback

The following are the benefits of getting an early and frequent feedback:

- **Risk mitigation through early and frequent feedback**
    - o Early and frequent feedback serves as a risk mitigation strategy, identifying issues and defects in the early stages of development.

    - It prevents critical bugs from reaching production environments, reducing potential impact on users and the business.
- **Enhanced code quality and software reliability**
    - Continuous feedback loops contribute to improved code quality and enhanced software reliability.
    - Early detection and prompt resolution of issues lead to more resilient software, resulting in better user experiences and fewer disruptions.
- **Agile iteration and faster feature release**
    - Rapid feedback empowers development teams to iterate and release features more quickly.
    - This agility allows teams to respond promptly to changing requirements, market demands, and emerging opportunities.
- **Collaboration and shared insights**
    - Feedback fosters collaboration among developers, testers, and stakeholders.
    - Shared insights create a common understanding of project goals and priorities, enhancing synergy, communication, and the collective pursuit of quality.
- **Data-driven decision-making**
    - Feedback provides data and insights crucial for decision-making.
    - Teams can prioritize tasks, allocate resources effectively, and make informed choices based on evidence and real-world observations.

Organizations implementing real-time feedback mechanisms can harness continuous improvement, reduce development risks, and deliver high-quality software that exceeds user expectations and market demands.

Implementing continuous improvement processes

In this subsection, we will implement continuous improvement processes within the context of CI/CD. We will discuss continuous improvement frameworks, methods for identifying areas for improvement, and the importance of RCA and corrective actions.

Continuous improvement frameworks

Continuous improvement is making incremental and ongoing enhancements to processes, practices, and outcomes. It is a fundamental principle in the world of CI/CD.

PDCA cycle

One of the most widely recognized continuous improvement frameworks is the PDCA cycle, also known as the **Deming** or **Shewhart Cycle**. Each phase of the PDCA cycle contributes to the iterative improvement process:

1. **Plan:** Teams initiate improvement efforts by setting clear objectives, identifying areas for change, and meticulously creating improvement plans. This planning phase ensures the organization has a well-defined path for the changes it wishes to implement.
2. **Do:** The implementation phase is where teams implement their plans. It involves executing the changes as per the improvement plan. Doing is the step where ideas are transformed into reality.
3. **Check:** The check phase involves evaluating the results of the implemented changes. It relies on measurement, analysis, and data collection to assess the impact of the changes on the overall system or process. This phase is crucial for understanding whether the changes have achieved their goals.
4. **Act:** Based on the evaluation results, teams take informed actions. These actions include making necessary adjustments to optimize processes or practices and standardizing improvements to ensure sustainability.

Identifying areas for improvement

To fine-tune CI/CD practices, incorporating continuous feedback mechanisms is pivotal. Let us explore key components and practices that contribute to ongoing improvement:

- **Continuous feedback:** Continuous feedback mechanisms play a pivotal role in identifying areas for improvement. Automated testing, monitoring, and user feedback are valuable sources of insights. They help in pinpointing issues and uncovering opportunities for enhancement.
- **Metrics and KPIs: Key Performance Indicators (KPIs)** and metrics provide quantitative measures of the CI/CD pipeline's performance, software quality, and delivery speed. These metrics clearly show how well the pipeline functions and signal deviations from desired performance levels.
- **Retrospectives:** Retrospectives are structured meetings where teams reflect on past work and collaboratively identify areas for improvement. These sessions encourage open communication and are commonly practiced in agile methodologies, such as *Scrum* and *Lean*. Retrospectives provide a dedicated space for team members to share their observations and insights.

Root cause analysis and corrective actions

To maintain a robust and effective CI/CD pipeline, the implementation of **root cause analysis (RCA)** stands as a pivotal practice. Let us understand the key aspects of RCA and its role in fostering continuous improvement:

- **RCA:** RCA is a structured approach to determine the fundamental reasons behind problems or issues. It goes beyond addressing symptoms and delves into the root causes that led to those symptoms. RCA is a crucial step in continuous improvement.
- **Techniques for RCA:** Several techniques facilitate root cause analysis, including the *5* **Whys** method, fishbone diagrams (**Ishikawa** diagrams), and fault tree analysis. These methods help teams dig deeper into the origins of issues and comprehensively understand the factors involved.
- **Corrective actions:** Once root causes are identified, teams can define and implement disciplinary actions or solutions to

address those causes. Prioritizing these actions and ensuring their effective implementation is essential. Corrective actions are instrumental in preventing the recurrence of problems.

- **Continuous monitoring:** Continuous improvement is an ongoing process. Teams must continuously monitor and follow up on implemented changes to ensure their effectiveness and sustainability. Monitoring helps identify any potential deviations or new issues that may arise.
- **Iterative improvement:** Continuous improvement is inherently iterative. Based on feedback and evaluation results, teams should regularly review and refine their improvement plans. This iterative approach ensures the CI/CD pipeline is continually optimized and aligned with evolving needs.

Organizations can systematically identify and address bottlenecks, inefficiencies, and issues in their CI/CD pipelines by implementing continuous improvement processes. This leads to more streamlined processes, improved software quality, and greater overall efficiency, all of which contribute to achieving continued delivery excellence.

Monitoring and metrics for performance optimization

This subsection delves into the importance of monitoring and metrics within CI/CD. We will discuss monitoring infrastructure and application performance, collecting relevant metrics, and utilizing metrics for optimization and decision-making.

Monitoring infrastructure and application performance

Monitoring is the essential practice of observing and tracking the behavior of infrastructure, applications, and services in real-time or near-real-time. It watches over the entire software delivery process. Infrastructure monitoring involves surveilling servers, databases, network devices, and containers. It ensures the availability, reliability, and performance of these critical elements of the CI/CD ecosystem. **Application performance monitoring** (**APM**) is a specialized form of monitoring that focuses on the behavior of applications. It measures critical aspects such as response times, error rates, and resource utilization. APM is invaluable for identifying bottlenecks, optimizing code, and improving application design. Monitoring should provide real-time data for immediate issue detection and historical data for in-depth trend analysis and long-term optimization. This combination of data sources offers comprehensive insights into system behavior.

Collecting relevant metrics

In the context of CI/CD and software development, there are various key performance metrics that need to be discussed, which are as follows:

- **Build and deployment times:** Measuring the time required for builds and deployments helps identify areas for optimization and efficiency gains.
- **Test coverage and test results:** Monitoring test coverage aids in assessing code quality, while tracking test results uncovers defects and validates functionality.
- **Infrastructure utilization:** Keeping tabs on CPU, memory, and storage utilization ensures efficient resource allocation and cost management.
- **Error rates and exceptions:** Measuring error rates and capturing exceptions is crucial for pinpointing software defects and stability issues.
- **User experience metrics:** Monitoring user interactions, page load times, and application responsiveness provides insights into user satisfaction and helps prioritize improvements.
- **Custom metrics:** Organizations should define and collect custom metrics tailored to their project needs and goals. These custom metrics may vary widely and can encompass anything from business-specific KPIs to project-specific performance indicators.
- **Data aggregation and visualization:** Data aggregation tools and visualization platforms (for example, Prometheus and Grafana) are instrumental in collecting, aggregating, and presenting metrics meaningfully. Dashboards and alerting rules can provide real-time visibility into system behavior.

Using metrics for optimization and decision-making

Collected metrics serve as a rich source of information for performance analysis. They can be analyzed to identify performance bottlenecks, resource constraints, and improvement areas. Techniques such as correlation analysis and anomaly detection aid in this process. Metrics play a pivotal role in capacity planning, which involves forecasting resource needs based on historical and current usage patterns. Teams can proactively scale infrastructure to handle increasing demand, ensuring optimal system performance. Metrics can trigger automated actions, such as auto-scaling to accommodate surges in user traffic or automatic rollbacks when error rates exceed predefined thresholds. These computerized responses enhance system resilience and reliability. Metrics should be at the heart of ongoing improvement efforts. Teams can set performance **objectives and key results (OKRs)** based on metrics, creating a data-driven approach to enhancement and optimization.

By implementing robust monitoring practices, collecting relevant metrics, and utilizing data for optimization and decision-making, organizations can significantly enhance the performance, reliability, and efficiency of their CI/CD pipelines, ultimately delivering high-quality software to end-users.

Ensuring data quality through data CI/CD

In this subsection, we will explore the crucial aspect of ensuring data quality within CI/CD. We will discuss data quality as an integral part of CI/CD, the implementation of data validation checks, and the automation of data quality assurance.

Data quality as a part of CI/CD

Data quality measures how well data meets the requirements and expectations of users and applications. It is paramount as accurate, complete, and reliable data is critical for effective decision-making and the proper functioning of software systems.

Data's role in CI/CD

Data plays a fundamental role in many applications, and its quality directly impacts software functionality and user experience. The concept of data CI/CD extends CI/CD principles to ensure the continuous delivery of high-quality data assets.

Data quality dimensions

Key dimensions of data quality include accuracy, completeness, consistency, reliability, and timeliness. These dimensions define the data quality and are assessed and monitored throughout the lifecycle.

Implementing data validation checks

Data validation involves automated checks and tests to verify data quality at every CI/CD pipeline stage. Integrating data validation into CI/CD enhances data reliability and usability.

Validation rules

Creating validation rules and checks specific to data quality requirements is essential. These rules can encompass regular expressions, business rules, and data profiling techniques to define comprehensive validation criteria. Business rules are essential part of development process and heavily rely on input from the business users. To develop these rules, a systematic procedure must be agreed upon between development teams and the business unit to govern and design rules specific to data values, contextual information, business terminologies, and so on.

Automated data validation tools

Various tools and frameworks facilitate computerized data validation, such as Apache Nifi, great expectations, or custom scripts integrated into the CI/CD pipeline. These tools streamline the validation process.

Validation metrics

Validation checks should produce metrics and reports that provide insights into data quality. Dashboards and alerts can be utilized to communicate data quality issues promptly, allowing for rapid corrective actions.

Automating data quality assurance

Ensuring constant data validation throughout the pipeline is crucial. Automated checks should run at every stage, from data ingestion and transformation to storage and consumption, guaranteeing data quality at all times. Data pipelines can be designed to cleanse and transform data when quality issues are detected automatically. This proactive approach ensures that data quality is maintained as data flows through the pipeline. Feedback loops are instrumental in data quality assurance. When data quality issues are identified, feedback mechanisms trigger corrective actions, including data correction, notifications to relevant stakeholders, or adjustments to the pipeline configuration. Treating data quality as a gate in the CI/CD pipeline is a best practice. If data does not meet predefined quality criteria, the pipeline can be halted or routed to remediation processes, preventing the propagation of low-quality data.

Conclusion

This chapter focused on optimizing CI/CD practices for large projects, diverse environments, and data quality. It explores strategies for handling complexity, managing codebases, and employing parallelization. Emphasis is placed on data CI/CD's role in managing large datasets. The nuances of different environments, from development to production, are discussed, highlighting challenges and strategies for harmonization. The chapter underscores continuous improvement through feedback loops and explores tools for monitoring, metrics, and software quality. It concludes by championing data quality and invites reflection on gained insights to refine CI/CD practices, navigate diverse environments, and continuously enhance software delivery.

In the next chapter, we will cover the dynamic landscape of CI/CD concerning mobile and the **Internet of Things** (**IoT**). The exploration will encompass strategies tailored to these specialized domains, shedding light on unique challenges and effective practices. Additionally, we will investigate the pivotal role of tools in achieving seamless, continuous delivery. The chapter will also cover best practices that contribute to the successful implementation of CI/CD across diverse environments and specific application domains.

CHAPTER 6
Specialized CI/CD Applications

Introduction

In this chapter, we will explore the different variations of **continuous integration and continuous delivery** (**CI/CD**) in mobile and **Internet of Things** (**IoT**) applications. We will also examine the specialized CI/CD practices essential for mobile app development, addressing version control, automated testing across devices, and the app store submission process. We will also tackle the unique challenges posed by IoT development, such as firmware updates and device compatibility while focusing on strategies that ensure robustness and reliability. Further, we will examine the role of CI/CD in delivering seamless user experiences despite the diversity of environments where mobile and IoT applications operate. As we transition into leveraging tools for continuous delivery, we will discuss the specialized tools and platforms that cater to the specific needs of mobile and IoT development, discussing customization, integration, and best practices to enhance efficiency. Finally, we will conclude with a detailed examination of the best practices for CI/CD across various industries. This will be supplemented by case studies of successful implementations, providing a comprehensive guide for delivering high-quality and reliable applications in rapidly evolving technological landscapes.

Structure

This chapter covers the following topics:

- CI/CD for mobile and IoT
- Leveraging tools for continuous delivery
- CI/CD best practices

Objectives

This chapter comprehensively explores continuous integration and CI/CD tailored specifically for mobile and IoT applications. Readers will understand the complexities of mobile app development, including version control, automated testing, and app store submissions. Additionally, this chapter will address the unique challenges in IoT development, such as firmware updates and device compatibility, while emphasizing strategies for ensuring robustness and reliability. Through a detailed examination of specialized CI/CD practices and tools, readers will learn to navigate the complexities of mobile and IoT development environments, covering customization, integration, and best practices for enhanced efficiency. The chapter offers an in-depth analysis of CI/CD best practices across industries, supplemented by case studies of successful implementations, providing readers with a valuable guide to delivering high-quality and reliable applications.

CI/CD for mobile and IoT

In mobile and IoT development, the advantages of CI/CD are manifold. Swift and reliable deployment of updates is paramount, particularly in mobile applications. For IoT devices, where reliability and performance are critical, CI/CD ensures that firmware and software updates are efficiently delivered to enhance functionality and address vulnerabilities. Let us discuss some of the specialized practices in the next section.

CI/CD practices for mobile app development

Mobile app development is a rapidly evolving field within broader software development. The unique characteristics of mobile devices, the diversity of platforms, and constantly changing user expectations create a set of distinct challenges that require specialized CI/CD practices. We will explore these challenges and the practices that can enhance the efficiency and reliability of the mobile app development lifecycle.

Version control for mobile projects

Version control is an integral part of the process of developing mobile applications. It helps to keep track of changes made to the code and makes collaboration between team members easier. Version control systems are essential for mobile projects as they help to reduce errors and allow applications to evolve. In this section, we will examine why version control is important in mobile development:

- **Mobile-first version control strategy:** Traditional version control systems might suffice for web or desktop applications, but mobile app development requires a more nuanced approach. A *mobile-first* version control strategy focuses on managing codebases specifically for mobile platforms. This involves maintaining separate repositories for iOS and Android development, enabling targeted updates, issuance of release notes, documentation and ensuring platform version parity. Popular version control tools like *Git* can be configured to accommodate this strategy effectively.
- **CI for Swift and Kotlin:** For iOS and Android development, respectively, Swift and Kotlin have become the dominant programming languages. Setting up CI pipelines to these languages is essential. CI servers can be configured to build and test Swift-based iOS apps using tools like *Fastlane* and *Bitrise,* while Kotlin-based Android apps benefit from integration with *Gradle* and *Android Studio*. There are some common tools like Jenkins for both types of devices to automate the build, testing, and deployment. This approach streamlines the build process and ensures early detection of code issues.

Automated testing on various devices and OS versions

As mobile technology advances, it is becoming increasingly important to ensure that mobile applications work seamlessly across various devices and operating systems. Automated testing is crucial in validating mobile apps on different devices and OS versions.

Developers can save time and improve app reliability by automating testing. Two key strategies stand out for optimizing the testing process within CI/CD pipelines are as follows:

- **Device and emulator farm integration:** Mobile app testing must encompass various device configurations, screen sizes, and OS versions. CI/CD pipelines should integrate with device farms or emulators to automatically run tests on a diverse set of environments. Tools like *Appium, Espresso,* and *XCTest* offer cross-platform compatibility and facilitate testing automation across iOS and Android.
- **Parallel testing for efficiency:** Mobile app testing can be time-consuming, especially when executed sequentially. Implementing parallel testing enables multiple tests to run concurrently, significantly reducing test execution time. This can be achieved by leveraging cloud-based testing services or setting up a testing grid that allows for simultaneous testing across different devices and OS versions.

Dealing with app store submissions and updates

When it comes to developing mobile apps, submitting and updating them in app stores can be a bit of a challenge. It is a crucial part of the development process, and it is essential to get it right. In this section, we will explore some strategies to make the deployment process more accessible so you can submit your app to app stores with ease and update it seamlessly. This applies to both mobile apps and their integrated IoT counterparts:

- App store submissions and updates are critical phases in the mobile app development lifecycle. To streamline app deployment, configure CI/CD pipelines for automatic release to app stores like the Apple App Store and Google Play Store. Automation not only saves time but also minimizes the risk of manual errors during submission, ensuring a smooth release process.
- In IoT, where mobile apps often serve as control interfaces for interconnected devices, **over-the-air (OTA)** updates play a pivotal role. Extending CI/CD pipelines to support OTA updates ensures a seamless mechanism for delivering updates

to IoT devices through the mobile app. This not only elevates the user experience by enabling hassle-free updates but also maintains the security posture of IoT devices, a critical consideration in the rapidly evolving landscape of connected technologies.

- Effectively navigating app store submissions and updates demands a strategic integration of automated deployment pipelines and OTA update mechanisms. By leveraging these approaches, developers not only ensure a smoother deployment process but also contribute to the resilience, security, and user-centricity of both mobile applications and their integrated IoT components.

Emphasis on speed, reliability, and efficiency

As we explore the complexities of specialized CI/CD practices for mobile app development, our primary focus is highlighting the fundamental principles of speed, reliability, and efficiency. The following principles will guide us through the crucial aspects that are required for a successful mobile app development lifecycle:

- **Speed:** Mobile users expect rapid updates and bug fixes. CI/CD pipelines that expedite the development process and enable frequent releases are crucial for meeting user demands.
- **Reliability:** Mobile apps must function flawlessly to maintain user trust. Rigorous testing, automated deployment, and error monitoring are critical components of a reliable CI/CD pipeline.
- **Efficiency:** Streamlining development workflows, minimizing manual intervention, and optimizing resource utilization contribute to overall project efficiency.

Mobile app development presents unique challenges that demand tailored CI/CD practices. By implementing version control strategies, automated testing, and efficient deployment processes, mobile app developers can meet user expectations for speed, reliability, and efficiency while handling the complexities of the mobile ecosystem. These practices not only improve the development lifecycle but also enhance the overall user experience of mobile applications.

IoT-specific CI/CD considerations and challenges

IoT development is a complex and rapidly evolving field that combines hardware and software components to create interconnected devices. Special considerations are needed for these devices in the context of CI/CD.

Here, we will explore the unique challenges and considerations for CI/CD in IoT development. Take a look at the following table:

In context of CI/CD	Challenge	Consideration
Firmware updates	IoT devices typically run on embedded firmware, which must be updated periodically to fix bugs, add features, or address security vulnerabilities. Managing these updates efficiently and securely is a significant challenge.	CI/CD pipelines for IoT should include firmware version control and automated deployment mechanisms. OTA updates are crucial for remotely updating device firmware. These updates should be thoroughly tested to ensure they do not disrupt the device's operation.
Device compatibility	IoT ecosystems often consist of diverse devices with varying capabilities, communication protocols, and hardware configurations. Ensuring compatibility and interoperability among these devices is a complex task.	IoT CI/CD pipelines should include extensive compatibility testing. This involves testing IoT applications across different device types, versions, and communication protocols to ensure seamless operation. Automated testing frameworks can help streamline this process.
Security	Security is a concern in IoT, as compromised devices can have severe consequences. IoT devices are often exposed to the internet, making them potential cyberattack targets.	Security should be integrated into every aspect of the CI/CD pipeline. This includes code reviews for security vulnerabilities, automated security testing, and secure update mechanisms for firmware. Additionally, device authentication and encryption should be implemented to protect data integrity and user privacy.

In context of CI/CD	Challenge	Consideration
Real-world testing	IoT devices often operate in unpredictable real-world environments. Testing solely in a controlled lab setting may not reveal all potential issues.	To address the mentioned challenge, IoT CI/CD pipelines should incorporate testing in real-world scenarios. This can involve simulating various environmental conditions, network disruptions, and device interactions. Crowdsourced testing with diverse user groups can provide valuable insights into real-world device behavior.
Automating deployments to edge devices	Many IoT devices operate at the network's edge, making traditional deployment processes challenging. Manually updating each device can be impractical and error-prone.	CI/CD for IoT should include automated deployment mechanisms that can push updates to edge devices efficiently. Technologies like Docker containers, edge computing platforms, and OTA update services can be leveraged to automate and streamline deployments.
Data integrity and privacy	IoT devices often collect and transmit sensitive data. Ensuring data integrity, privacy, and compliance with data protection regulations is essential.	IoT CI/CD pipelines should include data encryption during transmission and storage, secure authentication, and access controls. Privacy regulations such as **General Data Protection Regulation (GDPR)** and **Health Insurance Portability and Accountability Act (HIPAA)** are of utmost importance.

Table 6.1: *Challenges and considerations in CI/CD development*

Integrating hardware and software presents unique challenges in developing IoT systems. When implementing CI/CD practices for IoT, it is crucial to consider firmware updates, device compatibility, security, real-world testing, automated deployments to edge devices, and data integrity and privacy. By addressing these challenges with appropriate strategies and tools, developers can create robust and secure IoT applications that meet the demands of the rapidly evolving IoT technology.

Strategies for mobile and IoT applications delivery

Reliability is a cornerstone of both mobile and IoT applications. Users expect these applications to work seamlessly in various environments and under different conditions. Here, we will explore critical strategies to ensure the reliability of mobile and IoT applications.

Monitoring and error tracking

The following points cover the strategy, considerations for mobile application and IoT application, and benefits to ensure that the application's performance is monitored indefinitely:

- **Strategy:** Implement robust monitoring and error tracking systems that continuously monitor the application's performance and collect data on any errors or issues.
- **Mobile application consideration:** For mobile apps, integrate monitoring **software development kits** (**SDKs**) that capture key performance metrics and crash reports. Utilize tools like *Firebase Performance Monitoring, New Relic,* or *Sentry* to gain insights into app performance and errors.
- **IoT application consideration:** In IoT, implement remote monitoring of device health and connectivity status. IoT platforms like *AWS IoT, Azure IoT,* or *Google Cloud IoT Core* offer comprehensive monitoring capabilities.
- **Benefits:** Monitoring and error tracking provide real-time visibility into application behavior, enabling proactive issue detection and rapid response. This helps maintain high reliability by identifying and addressing problems promptly.

Rollback mechanisms

The strategy, consideration, and benefits of rollback mechanisms for both mobile applications and IoT applications are as follows:

- **Strategy:** Develop and implement rollback mechanisms that allow for a quick and safe return to a previously known good state in case of issues.
- **Mobile application consideration:** For mobile apps, this might involve version control for app updates. App stores often support staged rollouts, allowing developers to release updates and halt distribution if issues arise gradually.

- **IoT application consideration:** In IoT, consider implementing dual-image updates for device firmware. This enables a rollback to the previous firmware version if a new update introduces problems.
- **Benefits:** Rollback mechanisms provide a safety net, ensuring that applications can quickly revert to a working state if problems are detected after deployment, minimizing user disruptions.

Handling intermittent connectivity in IoT devices

Here are the strategies, considerations, and benefits for handling intermittent connectivity in IoT devices:

- **Strategy:** Developing strategies to handle intermittent or unreliable network connectivity is a common challenge in IoT environments.
- **IoT application consideration:** In IoT, devices may operate in remote or unstable network conditions. Implement local data buffering and synchronization mechanisms to ensure data is not lost when connectivity is temporarily unavailable. Use protocols like **Message Queuing Telemetry Transport** (**MQTT**) or **Constrained Application Protocol** (**CoAP**) that are designed for unreliable networks.
- **Benefits:** By addressing intermittent connectivity issues, IoT applications can continue to collect and transmit data even in challenging network conditions, enhancing reliability and data integrity.

Prioritizing user experience

The strategy, consideration and benefits for prioritizing user experience are given as follows:

- **Strategy:** Prioritize **user experience** (**UX**) as a central aspect of application reliability. A reliable application should not only function correctly but also provide a smooth and intuitive user experience.
- **Mobile application consideration:** Focus on responsive design, intuitive navigation, and fast load times for mobile apps. Continuously gather user feedback and conduct usability testing to refine the user interface.

- **IoT application consideration:** Design user interfaces that are user-friendly and accessible via mobile apps or web interfaces. Ensure that device interactions are intuitive and reliable.
- **Benefits:** Prioritizing UX ensures that users can easily interact with and trust the application, which in turn enhances user satisfaction and promotes long-term usage.

CI/CD contribution to reliability

The strategy, consideration, and benefits of CI/CD contribution to reliability goals are as follows:

- **Strategy:** Integrate CI/CD practices to support reliability goals: Automate testing, deployment, and monitoring to maintain a consistent and reliable application delivery pipeline.
- **Mobile and IoT application consideration:** Implement automated testing suites that cover various use cases, device configurations, and network conditions. Automate the deployment process to reduce human errors and ensure consistency.
- **Benefits:** CI/CD practices streamline development and deployment, allowing for frequent updates and rapid response to issues. This agility contributes to the overall reliability of mobile and IoT applications.

Delivering reliable mobile and IoT applications involves a combination of strategies such as proactive monitoring, robust error handling, rollback mechanisms, managing intermittent connectivity, and prioritizing user experience. By incorporating these strategies and integrating CI/CD practices, developers can create applications that consistently perform well, even in challenging and diverse environments, ultimately earning user trust and satisfaction.

Leveraging tools for continuous delivery

In this section, we will explore more on the tools used for continuous delivery and how these tools can be leveraged for CI/CD process.

Exploring specialized tools and platforms for CI/CD

CI/CD ensures the efficiency and reliability of mobile and IoT application development. Choosing the right tools and platforms for CI/CD is crucial to meet the unique requirements of these domains. In this section, we will examine various specialized CI/CD tools and platforms, providing an overview of popular options and discussing their customization potential and considerations.

Jenkins

The overview of Jenkins and how it can be customized to address more challenges is given as follows:

- **Overview:** Jenkins is one of the most widely adopted open-source CI/CD automation tools. Its extensibility and flexibility suit various development environments, including mobile and IoT.
- **Customization potential:** Jenkins can be customized for mobile and IoT development by integrating plugins and extensions tailored to these domains. For mobile, plugins like Fastlane enable automated iOS and Android app builds and deployments. For IoT, Jenkins can be configured to manage firmware updates and IoT-specific testing frameworks.
- **Considerations**
    - o **Cross-platform support:** Jenkins is versatile and compatible with various languages and OS.
    - o **Scalability:** Jenkins can be scaled horizontally to accommodate increased workloads, which is crucial when dealing with sizeable mobile apps or IoT device fleets.
    - o **Community support:** With a vast user community and an active developer ecosystem, Jenkins offers robust community support through forums, plugins, and documentation.
- **Pros**
    - o **Extensive customization:** Jenkins is highly customizable, allowing developers to tailor CI/CD pipelines to specific needs. This flexibility is crucial for addressing diverse challenges in mobile and IoT development.

- **Open-source and widely adopted:** Being open-source, Jenkins enjoys widespread adoption. Its large user base contributes to a rich ecosystem of plugins and extensions, ensuring compatibility with various tools and technologies.
- **Plugin ecosystem:** Jenkins supports a vast array of plugins, enabling seamless integration with different tools and platforms. For mobile development, plugins like Fastlane enhance automation for iOS and Android builds and deployments.
- **Cross-platform compatibility:** Jenkins is versatile and compatible with various programming languages and operating systems. This cross-platform support makes it suitable for diverse development environments.
- **Horizontal scalability:** Jenkins can be scaled horizontally to handle increased workloads. This scalability is essential for managing large mobile applications or fleets of IoT devices efficiently.
- **Active community support:** With a large and active user community, Jenkins benefits from robust community support. Users can access forums, plugins, and extensive documentation, providing solutions and insights for various challenges.

- **Cons**
  - **Learning curve:** The extensive customization and configuration options in Jenkins may result in a steep learning curve for new users. Teams may require time and effort to master its features.
  - **Maintenance overhead:** Managing Jenkins instances and plugins may require ongoing maintenance. Keeping plugins up-to-date and ensuring compatibility can introduce overhead.
  - **Resource intensive:** Jenkins can be resource intensive, particularly as the scale of CI/CD processes increases. Large builds or concurrent jobs may demand substantial server resources.
  - **User interface complexity:** The user interface, while feature-rich, can be complex. Navigating through

configurations and settings might be overwhelming for users unfamiliar with Jenkins.

- o **Limited built-in security:** Jenkins provides basic security features, but additional plugins or configurations may be needed for more advanced security requirements. It is crucial to address security considerations adequately.

In summary, Jenkins is a powerful and versatile CI/CD tool with extensive customization options and strong community support. However, teams should consider the learning curve, maintenance overhead, and resource implications when adopting Jenkins for their CI/CD pipelines.

Travis CI

The overview of Travis CI and how it can be customized to address more challenges is given as follows:

- **Overview:** Travis CI is a cloud-based CI/CD service that automates software builds and deployments. It is suitable for mobile and IoT projects hosted on platforms like *GitHub* and *Bitbucket*.
- **Customization potential:** Travis CI provides customization through configuration files (`.travis.yml`). For mobile development, you can define and build scripts that target specific platforms and environments. For IoT, Travis CI can be configured to perform firmware updates and device testing based on project requirements.
- **Considerations**
    - o **Cross-platform support:** Travis CI integrates seamlessly with popular version control platforms and provides versatile support for different programming languages and environments.
    - o **Scalability:** Travis CI offers cloud-based and self-hosted options, allowing teams to scale their CI/CD infrastructure according to their needs.
    - o **Community support:** Travis CI has an active community and extensive documentation to assist developers in setting up and optimizing their CI/CD pipelines.

- **Pros**
  - **Cloud-based service:** Travis CI operates as a cloud-based CI/CD service, eliminating the need for users to manage infrastructure. This cloud-centric approach simplifies setup and maintenance.
  - **Automation of builds and deployments:** Travis CI excels in automating software builds and deployments. This automation streamlines the development workflow, ensuring consistent and reliable processes.
  - **Configuration through .travis.yml:** Travis CI allows customization through a straightforward configuration file (`.travis.yml`). This YAML file simplifies the definition of build scripts, making it easy for developers to specify platform and environment requirements.
  - **Cross-platform support:** Travis CI integrates seamlessly with popular version control platforms and provides versatile support for various programming languages and environments. This cross-platform compatibility enhances its suitability for diverse projects.
  - **Scalability options:** Teams can choose between cloud-based and self-hosted options, providing scalability to adapt CI/CD infrastructure based on project needs. This flexibility is valuable for accommodating varying workloads.
  - **Active community support:** Travis CI boasts an active community, offering extensive documentation and support resources. Developers can seek assistance in forums and access documentation for setting up and optimizing CI/CD pipelines.
- **Cons**
  - **Limited customization compared to Jenkins:** While Travis CI offers customization through `.travis.yml`, it may have fewer customization options compared to more complex CI/CD tools like Jenkins. Teams with highly specific requirements may find limitations.
  - **Dependency on external platforms:** Travis CI's cloud-based nature means dependency on external servers. Users

should consider potential connectivity issues or service disruptions that could impact CI/CD processes.

- o **Self-hosted options require maintenance:** While self-hosted options provide scalability, they also introduce maintenance responsibilities. Teams opting for self-hosted solutions need to manage and maintain their CI/CD infrastructure.
- o **Learning curve for configuration:** Configuring Travis CI through `.travis.yml` may have a learning curve for users new to the system. However, this curve is generally less steep compared to more complex CI/CD tools.

In summary, Travis CI offers a cloud-based, automated CI/CD service with easy configuration through `.travis.yml`. It excels in cross-platform support and scalability, supported by an active community. However, users should be mindful of customization limitations and potential dependencies on external platforms.

CircleCI

The overview of CircleCI and how it can be customized to address more challenges is given as follows:

- **Overview:** CircleCI is a cloud-based CI/CD platform known for its simplicity. It is suitable for mobile and IoT development, offering automation for builds, testing, and deployments.
- **Customization potential:** CircleCI provides customizability through the `.circleci/config.yml` configuration file. Mobile projects can be customized to build and deploy apps for specific platforms and configurations. For IoT, CircleCI can be adapted to manage device deployments, OTA updates, and testing.
- **Considerations**
    - o **Cross-platform support:** CircleCI is compatible with various version control systems and programming languages, making it versatile for mobile and IoT projects.
    - o **Scalability:** CircleCI offers scalable cloud-based plans and customizable options for self-hosted infrastructure to accommodate growing development needs.

  - **Community support:** CircleCI boasts an active community, extensive documentation, and integrations with various third-party tools and services to enhance CI/CD pipelines.
- **Pros**
  - **Simplicity and user-friendly interface:** CircleCI is recognized for its simplicity and user-friendly interface, making it accessible to both beginners and experienced developers. The straightforward design contributes to a quick setup and easy navigation.
  - **Cloud-based CI/CD platform:** Being a cloud-based platform, CircleCI removes the burden of infrastructure management. Users benefit from automated builds, testing, and deployments without the need for extensive setup and maintenance.
  - **Customization through .circleci/config.yml:** CircleCI offers customization through the `.circleci/config.yml` configuration file. This `YAML` file allows users to define build and deployment processes, tailoring them to specific project requirements.
  - **Cross-platform support:** CircleCI is compatible with various version control systems and supports multiple programming languages, enhancing its versatility for mobile and IoT development. It accommodates diverse project setups seamlessly.
  - **Scalability options:** CircleCI provides scalable cloud-based plans, allowing teams to adapt their CI/CD infrastructure to evolving development needs. Additionally, customizable options for self-hosted infrastructure provide flexibility in scaling.
  - **Active community support:** CircleCI boasts an active community, comprehensive documentation, and integrations with various third-party tools and services. This support ecosystem enhances the platform's capabilities and assists users in optimizing their CI/CD pipelines.
- **Cons**
  - **Configuration complexity for advanced setups:** While CircleCI is known for simplicity, advanced configurations

in the **`.circleci/config.yml`** file might become complex for intricate setups. Users should be prepared for a learning curve when implementing sophisticated processes.

- **Dependency on external servers:** As a cloud-based platform, CircleCI relies on external servers. Users should consider potential connectivity issues or service disruptions impacting CI/CD processes.
- **Self-hosted infrastructure requires maintenance:** Teams opting for self-hosted infrastructure with CircleCI need to manage and maintain their infrastructure, which involves additional responsibilities.
- **Learning curve for advanced features:** Advanced features or intricate setups may require users to delve deeper into the platform's capabilities, potentially posing a learning curve for those seeking to utilize more complex functionalities.

In summary, CircleCI is a cloud-based CI/CD platform known for its simplicity, customizability, and scalability. It excels in cross-platform support, supported by an active community and extensive documentation. However, users should be mindful of potential configuration complexities for advanced setups and dependencies on external servers.

Azure DevOps

The overview of Azure DevOps and how it can be customized to address more challenges is given as follows:

- **Overview:** Azure DevOps is a part of Microsoft's Azure cloud ecosystem. It offers a comprehensive suite of CI/CD tools and services and is well-suited for both mobile and IoT projects.
- **Customization potential:** Azure DevOps provides customization through its pipelines, allowing you to define build and release tasks according to your specific mobile and IoT requirements. It is capable of supporting multiple programming languages and platforms, which makes it flexible enough to cater to different use cases.
- **Considerations**
  - **Cross-platform support:** Azure DevOps offers broad support for various development platforms, including

mobile app development (iOS, Android) and IoT (Azure IoT Hub, Azure IoT Edge).

 - **Scalability:** Azure DevOps is hosted on the Azure cloud platform, providing the required scalability to accommodate the growth of mobile and IoT projects.
 - **Community support:** As part of the Microsoft ecosystem, Azure DevOps benefits from a large user community, extensive documentation, and integration with other Microsoft services and products.

- **Pros**
  - **Comprehensive CI/CD suite:** Azure DevOps is part of Microsoft's Azure cloud ecosystem and offers a comprehensive suite of CI/CD tools and services. It provides an integrated environment for development, testing, and deployment.
  - **Customization through pipelines:** Azure DevOps allows customization through its pipelines, enabling users to define build and release tasks tailored to specific mobile and IoT requirements. This flexibility supports multiple programming languages and platforms.
  - **Cross-platform support:** Azure DevOps offers broad support for various development platforms, making it suitable for mobile app development (iOS, Android) and IoT (Azure IoT Hub, Azure IoT Edge). It accommodates diverse use cases with its cross-platform capabilities.
  - **Scalability with Azure cloud:** Being hosted on the Azure cloud platform, Azure DevOps provides scalability to accommodate the growth of mobile and IoT projects. Users can scale resources as needed, ensuring optimal performance for their CI/CD pipelines.
  - **Community support:** As part of the Microsoft ecosystem, Azure DevOps benefits from a large user community. Extensive documentation and integration with other Microsoft services and products contribute to robust community support.
  - **Integration with Microsoft services:** Azure DevOps seamlessly integrates with other Microsoft services

and products, creating a cohesive development and deployment environment for users already invested in the Microsoft ecosystem.

- **Cons**
  - o **Learning curve for new users:** Azure DevOps, with its comprehensive set of tools, may present a learning curve for new users. Mastery of the various features and functionalities might take time, especially for those unfamiliar with Microsoft's ecosystem.
  - o **Dependency on Azure ecosystem:** While beneficial for users within the Microsoft ecosystem, Azure DevOps relies on Azure services. Users heavily invested in alternative cloud platforms may find integration less seamless.
  - o **Configuration complexity:** Advanced configurations in pipelines may introduce complexity, requiring users to invest time in understanding and implementing intricate CI/CD processes.
  - o **Limited third-party integrations:** Compared to some other CI/CD tools, Azure DevOps may have limitations in terms of third-party integrations. Users should assess the availability of integrations relevant to their development stack.

In summary, Azure DevOps provides a comprehensive CI/CD suite with customization through pipelines, cross-platform support, scalability in the Azure cloud, and strong community support. However, users should be prepared for a learning curve, dependency on the Azure ecosystem, potential configuration complexities, and considerations regarding third-party integrations.

Xcode Server

Mobile CI/CD presents unique challenges and opportunities, especially in the context of iOS development. To address these, developers often leverage specialized tools such as Xcode Server for iOS. Mobile application development, particularly for iOS, requires a tailored CI/CD approach. The integration of continuous integration and continuous deployment practices helps streamline the development process, improve collaboration, and deliver high-quality mobile applications:

- **Overview:** Xcode Server plays a crucial role in the macOS application landscape, seamlessly integrating with Xcode, Apple's IDE. It is specifically designed to automate the building, testing, and deployment of iOS applications, making it an indispensable tool for iOS developers.
- **Customization potential:** Xcode Server offers remarkable customization potential through its seamless native integration within the Apple ecosystem. This integration ensures a unified and efficient experience for iOS developers, tightly coupled with Xcode, the primary IDE for Apple platforms. Notably, Xcode Server enables comprehensive testing, supporting various types like unit testing and UI testing for thorough assessments of iOS applications. Its robust continuous integration capabilities automate build and test processes, triggered automatically with code changes. The straightforward configuration process, especially for projects developed in Xcode, enhances its appeal, contributing to a streamlined and efficient CI/CD workflow tailored for iOS development.
- **Considerations**
    - **macOS dependency:** Xcode Server is dependent on macOS, restricting its use to Apple hardware. This dependency can pose a challenge for teams with diverse development environments.
    - **Limited cross-platform support:** While excelling in iOS development, Xcode Server may not be the optimal choice for cross-platform projects that extend beyond the Apple ecosystem.
    - **Scalability challenges**: Scaling Xcode Server can be challenging, particularly for larger teams or projects with complex requirements.
- **Pros**
    - **Native integration:** Xcode Server is tightly integrated with Xcode, Apple's IDE. This native integration provides a seamless experience for iOS developers within the Apple ecosystem.
    - **Comprehensive testing:** It supports various types of testing, including unit testing and UI testing, ensuring thorough testing of iOS applications. This contributes to the reliability of the CI/CD pipeline.

- **Continuous integration:** Xcode Server automates the build and test processes, triggering them automatically upon code changes. This continuous integration helps in maintaining code quality and catching issues early.
- **Easy configuration:** Setting up CI/CD pipelines with Xcode Server is relatively straightforward for projects developed in Xcode. The ease of configuration streamlines the onboarding process for developers.
- **Stability and reliability:** As a tool developed by Apple, Xcode Server benefits from the stability and reliability associated with Apple's software products. This can enhance the consistency of the CI/CD workflow.

- **Cons**
  - **macOS dependency:** Xcode Server is macOS-dependent, limiting its use to Apple hardware. This can be a constraint for teams with diverse development environments, especially those using non-Apple hardware.
  - **Limited cross-platform support:** While excellent for iOS development, Xcode Server may not be the best choice for cross-platform projects. It is specialized for Apple's ecosystem and may not cater to other platforms.
  - **Scalability challenges:** Scaling can be a challenge, especially for larger teams or projects with complex requirements. This limitation might affect the efficiency of the CI/CD pipeline as projects grow.
  - **Limited extensibility:** Compared to some cross-platform CI/CD tools, Xcode Server might have limitations in extensibility and integrations with non-Apple technologies.
  - **Dependency on Xcode:** The use of Xcode Server is closely tied to the Xcode IDE. Updates or changes in Xcode might impact Xcode Server, and users need to ensure compatibility with the latest Xcode versions.

In summary, Xcode Server offers strong native integration and testing capabilities for iOS development. However, its macOS dependency and limited cross-platform support should be considered based on the specific needs of the development team.

Exploring specialized tools and platforms for CI/CD in mobile and IoT development is essential for optimizing the development lifecycle. Jenkins, Travis CI, CircleCI, Azure DevOps and Xcode Server are versatile options that can be customized to meet the unique needs of these domains. The key considerations include cross-platform support, scalability, and the availability of community support and documentation to ensure the success of your CI/CD initiatives.

Evaluating and selecting the appropriate CI/CD tools and toolsets for specific application domains is crucial to meet their unique requirements and challenges. We will explore how to assess and choose the appropriate CI/CD tools based on the project's specific needs, including hardware and software dependencies.

Evaluating toolsets for specific application domains

Consider the following aspects for evaluating toolsets for specific applications domains. Let us discuss them in detail.

Identify domain-specific requirements

Before selecting CI/CD tools, it is essential to understand the requirements of the specific application domain thoroughly. Consider the following aspects for identifying domain specific requirements:

- **Hardware dependencies:** Identify the hardware components and devices that the application interacts with. Different domains may require specific tools to manage hardware integration, such as IoT devices, sensors, or specialized peripherals.
- **Software dependencies:** Determine the software libraries, frameworks, and platforms the application relies on. Some domains may have unique software dependencies, such as gaming engines for mobile game development or real-time operating systems for embedded systems in medical devices.
- **Regulatory compliance:** Consider any regulatory standards or compliance requirements specific to the domain. For example, medical IoT devices must adhere to strict regulations like HIPAA or FDA guidelines, which can influence the choice of CI/CD tools.

- **Performance and resource constraints:** Evaluate the performance and resource constraints of the target hardware. Certain domains, like IoT, may have limited processing power and memory, requiring tools that can optimize and minimize resource usage.
- **Integration to existing processes:** CI/CD tools are required to be integrated seamlessly with existing development, testing, and deployment processes. Sometimes, integration of CI/CD with legacy systems, which are usually not compatible with modern tools, requires extra effort. Organizations should evaluate whether a chosen tool allows for flexibility and easy migration to other tools if needed.

Assess tool capabilities

After identifying the domain-specific requirements, assess the capabilities of various CI/CD tools and toolsets. Consider the following factors to assess tool capabilities:

- **Compatibility:** Ensure that the tools you are considering are compatible with the hardware and software dependencies of your project. For example, if you are developing an Android game, you will need tools for Android app development and game engine integration.
- **Support for hardware integration:** If your project involves IoT devices or hardware peripherals, look for CI/CD tools that support hardware testing, provisioning, and deployment. Tools with built-in IoT device management capabilities can streamline the development process.
- **Security features:** Evaluate the security features of the tools. In areas such as medical IoT, ensuring security is of utmost importance. Ensure the selected CI/CD tools provide robust security measures, including code scanning, encryption, and secure update mechanisms.
- **Regulatory compliance support:** If your project falls under specific regulatory requirements, check if the CI/CD tools offer features or integrations that facilitate compliance. Some tools provide audit trails and documentation features that can simplify the compliance process.
- **Resource optimization:** Consider whether the CI/CD tools can optimize the use of hardware resources efficiently. For resource-constrained environments, tools that support lightweight builds and resource management are beneficial.

Evaluate tool ecosystem and integrations

Assess the ecosystem surrounding the CI/CD tools, including the availability of integrations and plugins. Consider the following to evaluate tools ecosystem and integrations:

- **Third-party integrations:** Look for tools with a rich ecosystem of integrations with third-party services, development platforms, and testing frameworks. This can streamline the CI/CD pipeline and extend functionality.
- **Community and documentation:** Evaluate the size and activity of the user community and the availability of documentation and support resources. A strong community can provide valuable insights and solutions to domain-specific challenges.
- **Customization and extensibility:** Check whether the tools allow for customization and extensibility. This is important for customizing the CI/CD pipeline to meet domain-specific requirements that out-of-the-box solutions may not cover.

Proof of concept and testing

Before making a final decision, consider conducting **proof-of-concept (PoC)** trials with the shortlisted CI/CD tools. Create a small-scale project representative of your domain's requirements and assess how well each tool performs in real-world scenarios. This allows you to validate the tool's suitability and identify potential challenges or limitations specific to your application domain.

Collaboration and team skillset

Consider the skillset and expertise of your development team. Choose CI/CD tools that align with the skills and knowledge of your team members. Training and familiarity with the selected tools can significantly affect the efficiency and success of your CI/CD pipeline.

Selecting the right CI/CD tools and toolsets for specific application domains involves thoroughly assessing domain-specific requirements, tool capabilities, ecosystem support, and team expertise. By carefully evaluating these factors, you can choose the tools that best align with the unique needs of your project, whether it is mobile game development, medical IoT devices, or any other specialized domain.

Tool integration is crucial for a successful CI/CD pipeline, as it streamlines the development workflow, improves collaboration, and ensures consistent and repeatable builds.

CI/CD best practices

CI/CD best practices are all about making software development faster, easier, and more reliable. To achieve this, it is recommended that developers automate certain processes, like building and testing, and integrate changes frequently. They should also keep track of different versions of their software and use automated deployment pipelines to ensure that everything runs smoothly. It is important to continuously monitor and provide feedback about how the software is performing. By following these best practices, developers can work together more effectively, reduce errors, and create high-quality software more quickly. Ultimately, this can help companies become more agile and better able to respond to changing requirements in software development.

Tool integration and best practices

Tool integration and best practices play a critical role in ensuring that the development process is efficient, collaborative, and of high quality. Tool integration is all about getting different software development tools to work together seamlessly, which in turn helps automate workflows, improve communication, and streamline the development pipeline. Some of the most common integrations include connecting version control systems, build tools, testing frameworks, and deployment automation tools. Meanwhile, best practices refer to a set of guidelines that ensure optimal performance, consistency, and quality in the software development process. These practices include using agile methodologies, continuous integration and delivery, and code reviews. By following the given best practices, software developers can build better products, faster and more efficiently.

Version control system integration

One of the key components of such a robust CI/CD pipeline is the integration of a **version control system** (**VCS**), which helps manage code changes and enables collaborative development. Git and Subversion are popular VCS systems that can be improved by following some best practices like:

- Use a VCS as the foundation of your CI/CD pipeline. Popular VCS options include Git (for example, *GitHub, GitLab, Bitbucket*) and Subversion.
- Establish a clear branching strategy, such as GitFlow or GitHub Flow, to manage code changes. This ensures that changes are tracked, reviewed, and merged effectively.

- Implement automated triggers to initiate CI/CD processes upon code commits or pull requests. Continuous integration should be tightly coupled with version control, ensuring every code change is built and tested.

Automated testing integration

The key strategies for integrating automated testing tools effectively, encompassing unit testing, integration testing, and end-to-end testing tailored to your application's specific requirements. The following aspects not only ensures the reliability of code changes but also promotes a proactive *test-first* approach:

- Integrate automated testing tools into the CI/CD pipeline. This includes unit testing, integration testing, and end-to-end testing, depending on your application's requirements.
- Implement a test-first approach by writing tests before developing new features or fixing bugs. This ensures that recent code changes do not introduce regressions.
- Use testing frameworks and libraries compatible with your programming language and development stack. Popular options include JUnit, Selenium, and pytest.

Containerization for consistent builds

Here are key strategies for effectively utilizing containerization in the development process:

- Containerize your application and its dependencies using technologies like Docker. Containerization ensures that the development and production environments are consistent, reducing the *it works on my machine* problem.
- Create a Dockerfile or equivalent configuration that defines the container image for your application. This file should specify the base image, installation of dependencies, and application deployment.
- Utilize container orchestration tools like *Kubernetes* or *Docker Compose* to manage containers in production. These tools facilitate scaling, load balancing, and fault tolerance.

Scripting and automation

Here, we will explore essential strategies for utilizing scripting and automation to enhance the repeatability and reliability of your CI/CD processes:

- Use scripting languages (for example, Bash, Python, PowerShell) to automate various aspects of the CI/CD pipeline, such as building, testing, deployment, and monitoring.
- Create reusable and maintainable scripts to perform everyday tasks. Avoid duplicating code by encapsulating functionality into functions or scripts that can be easily reused across multiple pipeline stages.
- Leverage CI/CD automation servers (for example, Jenkins, Travis CI) to schedule pipeline tasks. Automate the entire process from code integration to deployment to ensure consistency and reliability.

Continuous feedback and monitoring

By implementing mechanisms for instant feedback and establishing robust monitoring practices, development teams can swiftly respond to issues in both the development and production environments. Here, we will explore the essential strategies for integrating continuous feedback and monitoring seamlessly into your development workflow:

- Implement continuous feedback mechanisms to notify development teams of build and test results. Use tools like Slack, email notifications, or chat integrations to provide instant feedback.
- Set up automated monitoring and alerting systems to detect issues in production. Monitor key performance metrics, log data, and user feedback to identify and resolve problems promptly.
- Integrate feedback loops into the pipeline for code quality analysis, security scanning, and performance testing. Ensure that issues are addressed early in the development process.

Infrastructure as Code

Here, we explore the imperative strategies for adopting **Infrastructure as Code (IaC)**, ensuring consistency, traceability, and seamless automation of infrastructure changes within the CI/CD pipeline:

- Treat infrastructure as code by defining infrastructure components (for example, servers, databases, networking) in code using tools like Terraform, AWS CloudFormation, or Azure Resource Manager templates.

- Store infrastructure code in version control alongside application code to ensure consistency and traceability of infrastructure changes.
- Automate infrastructure provisioning and scaling as part of the CI/CD pipeline. Infrastructure changes should be validated, tested, and deployed automatically alongside application code changes.

Testing as code

In this section, we will cover the transformative strategies defining testing as code:

- Implement *testing as code* principles by automating the creation and management of test environments, data, and scenarios using scripts and configuration files.
- Use infrastructure automation and containerization to create disposable and reproducible test environments. Docker containers and container orchestration tools simplify the setup of isolated testing environments.
- Employ continuous testing, which means running automated tests continuously and incrementally as code changes are made, ensuring that testing remains an integral part of the development process.

Successful tool integration in the CI/CD pipeline relies on best practices such as version control system integration, automated testing, containerization, scripting and automation, continuous feedback, and treating infrastructure as code. These practices contribute to an efficient development workflow, leading to more reliable and consistent software deliveries.

Case studies

In this section, we will discuss real-world case studies.

GitHub's journey to CI/CD

Following are the challenges, strategies and benefits of GitHub's journey to CI/CD process:

- **Challenges:** GitHub needed to move from a deployment process that was manual and error-prone and took a full day of preparation to an automated CI/CD system.

- **Strategies**
  - o Adopted a ChatOps-driven deployment tool that developers could interact with via chat in GitHub.
  - o Moved towards smaller and more frequent deployments to reduce the risk associated with significant releases.
- **Benefits**
  - o Deployments went from once a week to multiple times a day.
  - o By automating their deployment process, they reduced the risk and fear of shipping new features and bug fixes.

Google's CI/CD pipeline for firebase

Following are the challenges, strategies and benefits of Google's CI/CD pipeline for firebase:

- **Challenges:** Google needed to maintain Firebase, a platform used by many mobile developers, and ensure it was robust, scalable, and consistently updated.
- **Strategies**
  - o Utilized Google Cloud Build to create a robust CI/CD pipeline.
  - o Implemented automated testing and deployment, enabling them to deploy changes rapidly.
- **Benefits**
  - o Reduced time to release new features.
  - o Improved the reliability and quality of each release.

IoT CI/CD pipeline of Bosch

Following are the challenges, strategies and benefits of IoT CI/CD pipeline of Bosch:

- **Challenges:** Bosch's **Cross Domain Development Kit (XDK)** needed a flexible and reliable CI/CD setup to manage its complex software that runs across a variety of IoT devices.
- **Strategies**
  - o Integrated Jenkins to automate the build and test processes.
  - o Leveraged Docker containers to ensure consistency across environments.

- **Benefits**
  - o Improved developer productivity by reducing setup times and making the build process more reliable.
  - o Enhanced the quality of their software through rigorous and consistent testing.

Wix's approach to mobile CI/CD

Following are the challenges, strategies and benefits of Wix's approach to mobile CI/CD:

- **Challenges:** Wix, a leading web development platform, wanted to ensure that its mobile app could be updated frequently with a high degree of automation.
- **Strategies**
  - o Developed a multi-branch development strategy, allowing features to be developed in isolation and merged into the main branch when ready.
  - o Emphasized the importance of testing, investing in a reliable suite of automated tests.
- **Benefits**
  - o The ability to deliver new features to users quickly and with confidence.
  - o Significant reduction in bugs reaching production due to the comprehensive test suite.

Etsy's evolution to continuous deployment

Following are the challenges, strategies and benefits of Etsy's evolution to continuous deployment:

- **Challenges:** Etsy needed to scale its deployment process to support a growing engineering team and a rapid development cycle.
- **Strategies**
  - o Transitioned from a biweekly release cycle to a continuous deployment model.
  - o Implemented a robust automated testing framework to validate changes before deployment to production.

- **Benefits**
  - o Deployments increased from twice a week to around 50 times a day.
  - o There was a notable improvement in developer productivity and morale, with developers able to see their work go live within hours.

To access some of these sources, especially papers and conference talks, you may need to go through industry conference archives or contact the organizations directly for their white papers. These case studies are a mixture of publicly available information and direct communications from the organizations at conferences and in their official publications.

Healthcare industry

Achieving CI/CD success can be challenging in different industries due to unique regulatory, security, and legacy system constraints. Here are practical tips and recommendations for CI/CD success in various industries:

- **Understand regulatory requirements:** Familiarize yourself with healthcare regulations such as HIPAA in the United States or GDPR in Europe. Ensure your CI/CD pipeline complies with these regulations by implementing robust data security and privacy measures.
- **Secure data handling:** Safeguard sensitive patient data by implementing encryption, access controls, and data anonymization techniques in development and production environments.
- **Perform regular security audits:** Conduct regular security audits and penetration testing to identify and address vulnerabilities proactively. Integrate security testing tools into your CI/CD pipeline to automate security checks.
- **Isolation of environments:** Maintain strict separation between development, testing, and production environments to prevent accidental exposure of patient data or disruption of healthcare services.

Automotive industry

In the automotive industry, software plays a vital role in ensuring safety, compliance, and performance. Here, we will explore critical strategies customized for the automotive sector, emphasizing safety-critical testing, regulatory compliance, simulation of real-world scenarios, and the need for continuous monitoring to uphold the integrity and reliability of vehicle software:

- **Safety-critical testing:** Prioritize safety-critical testing for vehicle software components. Implement automated testing for features like collision avoidance systems and autonomous driving algorithms.
- **Regulatory compliance:** Comply with automotive industry standards and regulations, such as ISO 26262, for functional safety. Integrate these requirements into your CI/CD pipeline, ensuring that software meets safety standards before deployment.
- **Test real-world scenarios:** Emulate real-world driving scenarios, including adverse weather conditions and complex traffic situations, in your testing environment to validate the reliability of automotive software.
- **Continuous monitoring:** Implement continuous monitoring of vehicle software in the field to detect and respond to issues promptly. OTA updates should be secure and rigorously tested.

Finance industry

The following key strategies safeguard the integrity and continuity of financial services in the CI/CD pipeline:

- **Regulatory compliance:** Adhere to financial regulations like **Payment Card Industry Data Security Standard (PCI DSS)** and GDPR, depending on your specific financial services. Automate compliance checks in your CI/CD pipeline to adhere to regulatory compliance.
- **Security first:** Make security a top priority in your CI/CD process. Perform code reviews, static code analysis, and security scanning to detect and mitigate vulnerabilities in financial software.
- **Rollback strategies:** Implement robust rollback strategies in case of unexpected issues during deployment. In the finance sector, downtime or errors can have significant financial consequences.
- **Disaster recovery plans:** Develop comprehensive disaster recovery and business continuity plans to ensure uninterrupted financial services during system failures or cyberattacks.

Government and public sector

The following key strategies are aimed at fostering transparent, secure, and inclusive government applications in the CI/CD pipeline:

- **Compliance with regulations:** Comply with government regulations and standards specific to your region, such as **Federal Information Security Management Act (FISMA)** in the United States or European GDPR. Implement audit trails and documentation to demonstrate compliance.
- **Security by design:** Incorporate security by design principles into your CI/CD pipeline. Regularly assess and update security policies to protect sensitive government data.
- **Citizen privacy:** Safeguard citizen privacy and data protection in all stages of development. Implement data encryption, access controls, and privacy impact assessments for government applications.
- **Accessibility:** Ensure that government services and applications are accessible to individuals with disabilities in compliance with accessibility standards such as **Web Content Accessibility Guidelines (WCAG)**.

Legacy systems

The following key strategies seamlessly integrate legacy systems into modern CI/CD pipelines:

- **Legacy modernization:** Consider strategies for modernizing legacy systems gradually. Implement microservices, containerization, or API gateways to enable integration with modern CI/CD pipelines.
- **Automated testing for legacy code:** Develop automated tests for legacy code to ensure that changes do not introduce regressions. Implement a testing strategy that covers critical components of the legacy system.
- **Documentation and knowledge transfer:** Document legacy systems thoroughly and provide knowledge transfer sessions for new team members. This facilitates smoother integration with CI/CD practices.
- **Incremental refactoring:** Refactor legacy code incrementally, focusing on high-impact areas. Break down monolithic applications into smaller components that are easier to manage within a CI/CD pipeline.

CI/CD success considers various industry-specific regulations, security concerns, and legacy systems. By following these practical tips and recommendations, organizations can navigate industry-specific challenges and leverage CI/CD practices to deliver software more efficiently and securely while ensuring compliance with industry regulations.

Conclusion

In conclusion, we explored specialized CI/CD applications with a particular focus on Mobile and IoT contexts. The readers gained insights into leveraging a diverse set of tools and adopting best practices tailored to these specialized domains. The chapter covers topics such as CI/CD for mobile and IoT, the effective use of tools for continuous delivery, and the implementation of CI/CD best practices. The readers are well-equipped to guide the unique challenges and opportunities presented by specialized CI/CD domains, promoting productivity, innovation, and excellence.

In the next chapter, we will explore real-world applications of CI/CD principles through a customized selection of case studies. These cases offer a practical and insightful examination of how various organizations and projects have successfully harnessed CI/CD to achieve remarkable outcomes.

References

1. **GitHub's journey to CI/CD:** The GitHub Blog provides insights into how their engineering team transitioned to CI/CD. The source is their official (blog post) (**https://github.blog/2015-06-02-deploying-branches-to-github-com/**).
2. **Google's CI/CD pipeline for firebase:** Details about Firebase's CI/CD processes have been discussed at various Google I/O events and in Google Developers' (blog posts) (**https://firebase.googleblog.com/**).
3. **IoT CI/CD pipeline of Bosch:** The IoT team at Bosch has presented their CI/CD approach at various tech talks and conferences, such as Jenkins World. Detailed documentation is also available on the Jenkins website (**https://www.jenkins.io/**) under user stories and case studies.
4. **Wix's approach to mobile CI/CD:** Wix Engineering has an official (engineering blog) (**https://www.wix.engineering/**) publishing articles about their processes and systems, including their CI/CD pipeline.

CHAPTER 7

Model Operations: DevOps Pipeline Case Studies

Introduction

In response to the growing adoption of **Machine Learning** (**ML**) in organizations, with 56% currently leveraging ML in at least one business function, the demand for streamlined DevOps practices has become imperative. The case study in this chapter explores the implementation of a DevOps pipeline for ML operations, providing insights into the strategies, tools, and techniques applied across various projects. The focus is on enhancing efficiency in ML model development and deployment, alongside measures taken for monitoring and maintaining models in production.

Structure

This chapter covers the following topics:

- Key considerations for the DevOps pipeline
- Case study: Building a DevOps pipeline for effective model operations
- Expanding CI/CD in MLOps pipeline

- Example: Bitbucket and Ansible Pipelines for CI/CD in Node.js
- Example: Implementing CI/CD on Azure
- Implementing CI/CD
- Testing stages in CI/CD
- Deployment methods
- Modification to database schema
- Outline of best practices

Objectives

This chapter provide a comprehensive understanding of key considerations in developing a DevOps pipeline for **Machine Learning Operations (MLOps)**. It encompasses model development, deployment, and monitoring with a focus on **continuous integration and continuous delivery (CI/CD)** aspects such as version control, automation, collaboration, and security in a cost-effective manner. This section aims to provide a holistic understanding of the collaborative efforts, data management strategies, and advanced technologies for sustainable ML model deployments.

Key considerations for the DevOps pipeline

Integrating a robust DevOps pipeline requires careful consideration across various domains. In this section, the key considerations to shape the foundation of a successful pipeline are explained:

- **Scope definition**
    - o Model development, deployment, and monitoring were identified as key areas.
    - o Additional considerations included:
        - ▪ **Version control:** Tracking model and code versions.
        - ▪ **Automation:** Reducing human error through task automation.
        - ▪ **Collaboration:** Ensuring effective teamwork across data scientists, engineers, and operations teams.

    - **Security:** Implementing access control measures.
    - **Costs:** Emphasizing cost-effectiveness in ML model deployment.

- **Technology landscape**
  - o Tailoring the DevOps pipeline to the client's infrastructure.
  - o Leveraging serverless services for efficient ML model deployments.
- **Cost and resource management**
  - o Addressing cost-related constraints:
    - Data storage costs are managed through AWS S3 buckets.
    - Evaluating licensing costs for third-party software.
    - Optimizing cloud service costs through serverless, on-demand services.
    - Considering human resources costs for specialized roles in ML operations.

Accessibility and governance

This section delves into the essential elements of access control, covering the fundamentals, implementation of authentication mechanisms, and the crucial aspects of data governance encompassing data quality, privacy, and compliance. These elements collectively contribute to the success of a DevOps pipeline for ML operations:

- **Access controls**
  - o Implementing authentication and authorization mechanisms.
  - o Ensuring only authorized users have access to deployed models and predictions.
- **Auditing**
  - o Keeping track of user access for compliance, security, and issue troubleshooting.
- **Monitoring**
  - o Continuous monitoring of deployed model performance for expected functionality and issue detection.

- **Code versioning**
  - o Preserving all previous versions of the deployed model for easy rollback if necessary.
- **Data governance**
  - o Emphasizing proper governance of data used for training, testing, and predictions.

Addressing data quality, privacy, and compliance, especially as deployments scale.

- **ML model explainability**
  - o Ensuring interpretability and understanding of the ML model by developers and stakeholders.
  - o Quantifying the value addition provided by the model.
- **Documentation**
  - o Maintaining detailed documentation of the deployed model, including architecture, training data, and performance metrics.
- **Security measures**
  - o Implementing security measures to protect models and predictions from unauthorized access and malicious attacks.

In conclusion, this case study outlines a holistic approach to building a DevOps pipeline for ML operations, emphasizing collaboration, cost-effectiveness, and robust governance for successful and sustainable model deployment in production environments.

Case study: Building a DevOps pipeline for effective model operations

In modern software development, the intersection of DevOps and ML has become a crucial focal point. This topic delves into a comprehensive case study showcasing the development of a robust DevOps pipeline tailored for effective model operations. The narrative unfolds within a compelling project aimed at detecting and managing fraud claims for a major insurer.

Project background: Detecting and managing fraud claims for a major insurer.

Problem statement: Our deployment focused on combating claims fraud for a major insurer, addressing the limitations of traditional manual review methods. Manual investigations were time-consuming, expensive, and prone to human error. In response, we developed an automated fraud detection and alerting system utilizing insurance claims data. This system leveraged advanced analytics and classic ML algorithms to identify patterns and anomalies indicating potential fraud.

The primary objective was to detect fraud early and accurately, minimizing the financial impact on the insurer and its customers. Our activities spanned the following steps:

1. Identifying data sources
2. Collecting and integrating data
3. Developing analytical/ML models
4. Integrating these components into a cloud environment
5. Utilizing the cloud for automation
6. Ensuring the deployment's robustness and scalability

Project team composition: The project involved a compact team of 6+ individuals, given as follows:

- **Two data scientists:** Responsible for ML model training and experimentation pipelines.
- **One data engineer**: Tasked with cloud database integration, collaborating closely with our cloud expert.
- **One cloud expert (AWS):** In charge of setting up the cloud-based systems.
- **One experienced UI developer (JavaScript/React):** Creating an intuitive ReactJS-based UI.
- **One business analyst:** Capturing client requirements.
- **Project lead (senior data scientist):** Oversaw model development and managed project aspects.

  Despite its seemingly small size, the team successfully developed several APIs for seamless integration into the backend application.

Activities in the model deployment process: As outlined in the problem statement, our actions were guided by the following steps:

1. **Sourcing and preparing the data**
   a. Emphasizing the importance of high-quality data by following the principle of *Garbage in, garbage out.*
   b. Introducing the concept of **Extract, Transform, Load (ETL)** for data warehousing.
   c. Highlighting the role of ETL pipelines in transforming and storing data from various sources.
2. **Sourcing the data**
   a. Data provided by the client, a product-based organization, sourced from relational databases, simple storage locations, and so on.
   b. Building ETL pipelines using AWS services for data transformation and storage.
   c. Utilizing specific AWS-managed services like DataPipeline, Kinesis Firehose, and so on.
3. **Data ingestion and transformation with AWS Glue**
   a. Detailing the process of creating an ETL pipeline using AWS Glue.
   b. Several key steps are involved in setting the pipeline, including creating a crawler, viewing the table, and configuring the job.
   c. Discussing the advantages of serverless services, such as AWS Glue, for triggered, cost-efficient data processing.
4. **Diverse data sources and transformations**
   a. Addressing the complexity of diverse data sources and transformations.
   b. Employing a combination of approaches, including multiple independent data pipelines and Python-based Lambdas for specific tasks.
   c. Managing data from streaming sources, images, and structured data from on-prem servers through customized pipelines.

In summary, our project developed a robust fraud detection system and showcased the importance of a well-orchestrated DevOps pipeline. The collaborative efforts of a diverse team, efficient data management strategies, and the implementation of advanced technologies contributed to the success of our CI/CD MLOps pipeline for insurance claims fraud detection.

Collaborative development and version control

In modern software development, version control is pivotal for tracking changes to code over time. Git is a distributed version control system in the software industry. In our AWS-powered project, we seamlessly integrated AWS CodeCommit, a fully managed version control service. Utilizing the Git version control system, CodeCommit provided a centralized repository for collaborative development, enabling developers to track and manage code changes efficiently. Establishing a comprehensive CI/CD pipeline is easier due to native integration with other AWS services, like CodePipeline and CodeBuild.

Computing environment

As we progressed through the project, the need for a robust computing environment became evident. While considering on-premise and cloud options, we opted for an **AmazonWeb Services Elastic Compute Cloud (AWS EC2)** instance to ensure a robust and highly available deployment. Contemplating factors such as total cost, we chose on-demand EC2 instances, paying only for the hours with no long-term commitments. This approach proved ideal for our project, with short-term, irregular workloads, and contributed to cost efficiency.

To elaborate further on the justification for choosing AWS EC2, its impact on performance and latency is noteworthy. AWS EC2 provides a dynamic and scalable infrastructure that allows us to easily adjust computing resources in response to changing project requirements. This scalability ensures optimal performance by efficiently handling fluctuations in workloads, allowing us to scale up or down as needed. The on-demand nature of EC2 instances aligns seamlessly with our project's variable workloads, enhancing cost efficiency while still meeting performance demands.

Additionally, AWS EC2's distributed infrastructure across multiple availability zones enhances the deployment's overall availability.

This distributed architecture minimizes the risk of downtime and improves reliability, crucial factors for a project with high availability requirements. Furthermore, the global reach of AWS helps reduce latency, ensuring that end-users experience minimal delays when accessing our application or services hosted on EC2 instances.

Operationalizing AWS EC2

Operationalizing AWS EC2 is a process of making AWS Elastic Compute Cloud instances fully operational and integrated into an organization's infrastructure. This involves configuring, managing, and optimizing EC2 instances to meet specific operational requirements:

- **Launch an EC2 instance:** Accessed through the EC2 console, allowing selection of instance type, choice of **Amazon Machine Image (AMI)**, and configuration of settings like security groups and key pairs.
- **Connecting to the instance:** Utilized **remote desktop protocol (RDP)** for Windows instances and **Secure Shell (SSH)** for Linux instances.
- **Install and configure software/packages:** Install and configure necessary software on the EC2 instance to set up the ML modeling environment.

Leveraging MLflow for model experimentation and tracking

With the computing environment ready, the next step was creating an environment for ML model experimentation. Despite the initial consideration of AWS SageMaker, we opted for MLflow, a vendor-agnostic, open-source framework that offered greater flexibility and control over ML workflows. The key considerations and features included:

- **Vendor-agnostic and open source**
    - o MLflow's flexibility across ML frameworks, cloud providers, and deployment platforms.
- **Experiment tracking**
    - o Robust tools within MLflow to track experiments, enabling performance monitoring and model version comparisons.

Setting up MLflow on EC2

Following are the steps on setting up MLflow on EC2:

1. **Installation**
    a. Executed `pip install mlflow` in the terminal to set up MLflow on the EC2 instance.
2. **Customizing MLflow for tracking**
    a. Developed a framework and custom code for the training/retraining pipeline, utilizing MLflow's experiment tracking capabilities.
3. **MLflow features leveraged**
    a. Utilized MLflow tracking API for logging experiments, metadata, artifacts, code versions, and results of Machine Learning experiments.
    b. Employed MLflow's model registry for a centralized repository to store and share models.
    c. Leveraged MLflow's ability to package code into reproducible runs.

In conclusion, integrating collaborative development, version control, and MLflow for model experimentation enriched our CI/CD MLOps pipeline, fostering efficient collaboration, reliable version control, and streamlined ML workflows.

Expanding CI/CD in MLOps pipeline

Now that we have prepared our data, established a computing environment, and set up the model experimentation and tracking server, the subsequent focus is on configuring the MLOps pipeline. Having completed data collection, model building, and experimentation, the logical progression involves model evaluation, deployment, monitoring, version control, and implementing CI/CD pipelines. The following high-level steps illustrate how these components were integrated into our MLOps pipeline:

Introduction to AWS tools for CI/CD

Before delving into the pipeline implementation, let us briefly introduce the AWS tools, many of which are serverless, facilitating the development of our CI/CD MLOps pipeline:

- **CodeCommit:** A fully managed version control service that serves as a centralized repository for source code. In our project, CodeCommit acted as the remote project repository.
- **CodeBuild:** A fully managed build service used for compiling, testing, and packaging code. Integrated seamlessly with CodeCommit, automating builds triggered by code changes.
- **CodeDeploy:** Another fully managed deployment service automating the deployment process to various environments. In our case, it facilitated the deployment to AWS EC2 instances.
- **CodePipeline:** An AWS service providing a visual interface for pipeline management. Orchestrated each step in the release process, integrating seamlessly with other AWS services.

The following steps illustrate how these components were integrated into our MLOps pipeline:

1. **Git installation:** Developers installed Git on their local systems by visiting `git-scm.com`.
2. **CodeCommit repository setup:** A new repository was created for the project, and developers cloned it locally using SSH/HTTPS.
3. **Build and test locally:** Local build and testing activities were carried out before committing changes to the CodeCommit repository.
4. **Front end/UI development:** Rigorous React JS-based UI/API testing was performed locally before pushing changes to the remote repository.
5. **Pull requests and code review:** Developers created pull requests proposing changes, with senior developers/code reviewers overseeing the merge process to the master branch.
6. **Setting up MLflow:** Discussed in the previous section, MLflow was integrated for experimentation and tracking.
7. **Master repository cloning to EC2:** The master repository in CodeCommit was cloned to the EC2 instance environment, where Python code for the ML application backend was

executed. This triggered a series of ML model experiments, selecting the best model for production staging.

8. **CodeBuild execution:** Triggered CodeBuild to compile, test, and package the code.
9. **CodeDeploy deployment:** If the build was successful, CodeDeploy was triggered, automating code deployment to the target environment (for example, AWS EC2).
10. **CodePipeline orchestration:** Leveraged CodePipeline for managing the pipeline, providing a visual interface for visibility into each stage's status.
11. **CodePipeline integration:** Integrated other AWS services into CodePipeline, orchestrating the software delivery pipeline.

AWS Sagemaker consideration

Despite the popularity of AWS SageMaker for ML model deployments, our project opted against it for the following reasons:

- **Higher usage cost:** SageMaker's usage costs were found to be higher, considering factors such as instance types, deployed model size, and data transfer.
- **Convenience of traditional deployment:** For our application with a JavaScript-based front end and Python ML-based backend, a conventional EC2 instance deployment proved more convenient.
- **Ease of operationalization:** Traditional deployment on an EC2 instance was deemed easier to operationalize using AWS CodePipeline.
- **Customization needs:** SageMaker's limitations in customizing the environment and accessing the underlying operating system led to the decision of not using AWS Sagemaker.

Model testing and monitoring

Model testing and monitoring is a crucial phase of ML that involves evaluating the performance, and robustness of a trained model. Follow the given steps:

1. **Metrics for model testing:** In fraud detection, critical metrics included recall and model lift. A lift chart visualizing model performance was employed to compare predictions with actual

outcomes. To add quantification to our data quality validation, we incorporated data profiling metrics such as identifying outliers, tracking higher missing percentages, and assessing data completeness. This allowed us to quantify the extent of data quality and identify potential areas for improvement.

2. **Addressing data drift:** To counter data drift, we focused on a comprehensive approach, encompassing data quality validation, model performance monitoring, and drift evaluation and feedback. In addition to regular checks for data drift, we implemented specific data profiling metrics to quantify shifts in data characteristics. This involved continuous monitoring of features for changes in statistical properties, enabling us to detect and address issues promptly. AWS CloudWatch played a pivotal role in logging events, including data quality metrics, and issuing notifications based on predefined thresholds.

Apart from the aforementioned steps, additional measures were implemented to enhance deployment robustness:

- **Analyzing model errors and patterns:** We conducted in-depth analysis of model errors and patterns to identify areas for improvement. By quantifying error rates and understanding the patterns of misclassifications, we fine-tuned our models to enhance overall accuracy and reliability.
- **Comparing production model performance with a benchmark model:** A/B testing was employed to compare the performance of the production model with a benchmark model. This approach provided a quantitative measure of improvements and validated the effectiveness of model enhancements over time.
- **Real-time monitoring for prompt issue detection:** Real-time monitoring, facilitated by AWS Lambdas, allowed for immediate issue detection and response. This proactive approach ensured that any anomalies or deviations from expected behavior were addressed promptly to maintain model performance.
- **Bias detection tests and feature importance tests:** We incorporated bias detection tests to identify and mitigate any biases in model predictions. Additionally, feature importance tests were performed to quantify the impact of individual features on model performance, providing insights for ongoing model evaluation and refinement.

All tests and monitoring, including the added data profiling metrics, were encapsulated in AWS Lambdas and triggered on demand or through scheduling, ensuring a comprehensive and quantifiable approach to model testing and monitoring.

Other CI/CD pipeline development aspects

As we delve deeper into the intricacies of building a robust CI/CD MLOps pipeline, this section explores additional aspects beyond the foundational steps. From the tools employed in code building to the collaborative coding environments and concluding reflections, we unravel the nuanced layers that contribute to an efficient and reliable ML deployment process.

Join us in examining the role of local development environments, cloud-based IDEs, and the continuous pursuit of optimization in CI/CD for ML:

- **Code building IDEs:** While AWS services played a vital role in the CI/CD pipeline, much of the code for model building was developed locally using PyCharm. PyCharm was chosen for its clean interface, code editing, debugging tools, project management features, and customization options.
- **Cloud 9 (AWS Managed Service):** AWS Cloud9 is a cloud-based IDE facilitating collaborative coding by providing a browser-accessible, fully managed environment. This allowed for easy code editing and collaboration among multiple users, offering integrated tools for code completion, debugging, and version control. Cloud9 eliminated the need for local IDE installations and configurations.

Building a CI/CD MLOps pipeline using AWS services, MLflow, and open-source tools significantly enhances the efficiency and reliability of ML deployments. AWS services like CodePipeline, CodeBuild, CodeDeploy, and MLflow contribute to automating the building, testing, and deployment of models, streamlining processes, and ensuring consistency.

While the pipeline presented is robust, developers can further enhance it by implementing monitoring and automation tools for real-time issue detection and performance improvement. Exploring Amazon SageMaker's scalable ML model deployment capabilities can provide a comprehensive solution for managing ML models at scale.

In conclusion, with the right tools and strategies, organizations can leverage AWS services and open-source tools to establish a streamlined, efficient, and reliable CI/CD MLOps pipeline. This optimization process can significantly improve the ML deployment process, delivering greater customer value.

Example: Bitbucket and Ansible Pipelines for CI/CD in a Node.js

Come along on a journey as we explore the world of automation in CI/CD. We will cover the basics, learn how to make deployments easy, set up pipelines for smooth integration, and understand the powerful impact that automation has on modern software development.

Introduction: Navigating the landscape of automation

In modern software development, the integration of robust automation tools is paramount. Ansible is a well-known tool for its prowess in automation, becomes a linchpin in server administration tasks. Complemented by Bitbucket Pipelines and functioning as Docker containers, this case study delves into their synergy by addressing their collaborative role in achieving continuous delivery for a Node.js project.

Orchestrating effortless deployments

The beauty of automating the deployment of a Node.js project lies in enhancing efficiency and reducing errors in critical tasks. Whether code updates, dependency management, database migration, or server restarts, Ansible provides the precision to define deployment tasks. Concurrently, Bitbucket Pipelines configures and launches Docker containers for seamless deployment.

Consider the refined Bitbucket Pipelines configuration (**`bitbucket-pipelines.yml`**) tailored for a Node.js project:

```
# use the official Node.js 14 docker image
   image: node:14

   pipelines:
```

```
branches:
  # deploy only when pushing to the main branch
  main:
    - step:
        name: deploy to prod    #Bitbucket deployment
        name
        deployment: Production
        caches:
          # cache the Ansible installation
          - npm
        script:
          # install Ansible
          - npm install -g ansible
          # go into the ansible directory
          # in this same repository
          - cd ansible
          # perform the actual deploy
          - ansible-playbook -i ./hosts deploy.yaml
```

This configuration specifies that the Node.js docker image is utilized, triggering deployments in the main branch. It considered caching of Ansible installation to save build time.

Setup your pipelines: Crafting a seamless integration

Follow the given steps:

1. **Add the bitbucket-pipelines.yml file to the repository's root**
   a. Create a file named `bitbucket-pipelines.yml` at the root of your repository. This file defines the configuration for Bitbucket Pipelines, specifying the steps to be executed during the CI/CD process.
   b. An example for a Node.js project is as follows:

```
# use the official Node.js 14 docker image
image: node:14
```

```
pipelines:
  branches:
    # deploy only when pushing to the main
    branch
    main:
      - step:
          name: deploy to prod    #Bitbucket
          deployment name
          deployment: Production
          caches:
            # cache the Ansible installation
            - npm
          script:
            # install Ansible
            - npm install -g ansible
            # go into the ansible directory
            # in this same repository
            - cd ansible
            # perform the actual deploy
            - ansible-playbook -i ./hosts
            deploy.yaml
```

Adjust the content based on your project's requirements and structure.

2. **Configure repository settings for Bitbucket Pipelines**
   a. Navigate to your **Bitbucket** repository on the web.
   b. Click on **Settings** in the left-hand menu.
   c. Under **Pipelines**, ensure that the feature is enabled for the repository.
3. **Under PIPELINES settings, generate SSH key pairs for Ansible's SSH connection**
   a. In the repository settings, find the **SSH keys** section under **PIPELINES**.

   b. Click on **Generate keys** to create a new **SSH key** pair.
   c. This key pair will be used for secure communication between Bitbucket Pipelines and your deployment server.

4. **Add the server's fingerprint to Known Hosts**
   a. Obtain the fingerprint of your deployment server. This is available in the server's SSH configuration or can be retrieved using the **`ssh-keyscan`** command.
   b. In the **SSH keys** section of repository settings, scroll down to Known Hosts.
   c. Insert your server's hostname in the **Host** address field.
   d. Press the **Fetch** button to obtain the fingerprint.
   e. Finally, click the **Add Host** button to add the server to the Known Hosts.

5. **Test the deployment by pushing changes to the main branch**
   a. Make changes to your code and push them to the main branch.
   b. Observe Bitbucket Pipelines automatically triggering the deployment pipeline defined in the **`bitbucket-pipelines.yml`** file.
   c. Monitor the pipeline execution in the Bitbucket interface.

6. **Utilize [skip-ci] in commit messages to prevent automatic deployment if needed**
   a. If you want to make changes to the main branch but prevent automatic deployment, include [**`skip-ci`**] in your commit message.
   b. For example, **`git commit -m "Fixing a bug [skip-ci]"`**.
   c. This ensures that the CI/CD pipeline will not be triggered for this commit.

This case study stands testament to a potent setup for continuous delivery in a Node.js project through the symbiosis of Bitbucket Pipelines and Ansible. The deployment process can be automated with technology to save time and decrease errors.

Automated deployment of Node.js with Ansible

If you are new to deploying Node.js on a production server, consider reading Node.js – NGINX: deploy your Node.js project on a production server for a basic introduction to the required steps. Setting up a VPS, configuring SSH access, installing and configuring essential software, creating a database user, and configuring Node.js can be time-consuming. By automating this process, you can save a significant amount of valuable time:

1. **Setup SSH access to your VPS**

   a. Choose a VPS provider (for example, DigitalOcean) and purchase a Debian/Ubuntu-based VPS with root SSH access.

   b. Configure SSH access in your local environment.

      # Example SSH configuration in **~/.ssh/config**

      Host: **yourserver**

      User: **root**

      Port: **22**

      HostName: **yourserver.example.com**

      Set up password-less access using SSH keys.

      # Generate SSH key pair

      ssh-keygen -t rsa -b 4096 -C "your_email@example.com"

      # Configure password-less access

      ssh-copy-id root@yourserver.example.com

2. **Deploy your Node.js project with Ansible**

   a. Clone the template repository for Node.js.

      ```
      git clone https://github.com/example/nodejs-ansible-deploy.git
      cd nodejs-ansible-deploy
      ```

   b. Customize Ansible Playbooks in the **Ansible** directory as needed.

c. Update the **Hosts** file with your server's information.

```
[yourserver]
yourserver   ansible_ssh_host=yourserver.example.
com ansible_ssh_user=root
```

Execute Ansible Playbooks to configure the server and deploy your Node.js project:

```
ansible-playbook -i hosts ansible/system.yaml
ansible-playbook -i hosts ansible/packages.yaml
ansible-playbook -i hosts ansible/config_files.yaml
ansible-playbook -i hosts ansible/postgresql.yaml
ansible-playbook -i hosts ansible/deploy.yaml
```

During the process, Ansible performs tasks such as setting up necessary packages, configuring NGINX and uWSGI, creating a PostgreSQL database, and deploying your Node.js project.

3. **Update your Node.js project**

   a. Push changes to your Git repository.

   ```
   git push origin master
   ```

   b. Run the Ansible playbook to update your Node.js project on the server.

   ```
   ansible-playbook -i hosts ansible/deploy.yaml
   ```

   c. The playbook fetches the latest changes from your repository, updates dependencies, migrates the database, collects static files, and restarts uWSGI.

4. **CD using Bitbucket Pipelines**

   a. Push changes to your Bitbucket repository to trigger Bitbucket Pipelines.

   b. Configure Bitbucket Pipelines to use Ansible for continuous delivery.

   ```
   # bitbucket-pipelines.yml
   image: python:2.7.16
      pipelines:
        branches:
   ```

```
master:
  - step:
      name: Deploy to Production
      caches:
        - pip
      script:
        - pip install ansible==2.8.0
        - cd ansible
        - ansible-playbook -i ../hosts
        deploy.yaml
```

This comprehensive guide demonstrates an automated deployment process for a Node.js project using Ansible. By automating repetitive tasks, you can save time and prevent errors in the deployment process. CD with Bitbucket Pipelines enhances your project's efficiency and reliability, ensuring seamless updates and improved development workflows.

Example: Implementing CI/CD on Azure

This example delves into Azure's CI/CD capabilities, showcased through a suite of developer services – Azure DevOps Services, Azure Repos, Azure Pipelines, Azure Artifacts, and Azure Deploy. These services empower developers and IT operations professionals practicing DevOps to securely and rapidly deliver software. The seamless incorporation of version control into an application's source code ensures secure storage and application of changes, contributing to an efficient and reliable software delivery process.

Complexity of software delivery

In today's dynamic business environment, enterprises confront the challenges posed by swiftly evolving competitive scenarios, ever-changing security demands, and achieving scalable performance. It becomes crucial for enterprises to bridge the gap between operational stability and the rapid development of features. Adapting CI/CD emerges as a strategic practice, facilitating agile software changes while ensuring system stability and security.

After recognizing the need for innovative approaches to meet the diverse business needs of its clientele, Azure realized that delivering features required groundbreaking software delivery methods. Navigating the expansive realm of Azure, seamless collaboration among numerous independent software teams is imperative. These teams work concurrently to deliver software swiftly, securely, reliably, and with zero tolerance for outages.

In the pursuit of achieving high-velocity software delivery, Azure and other visionary organizations have pioneered the principles of DevOps. DevOps combines cultural philosophies, practices, and tools to improve app and service delivery speed. Organizations can evolve and enhance products more rapidly by adhering to DevOps principles instead of traditional software development and infrastructure management processes. This increased speed enables companies to serve their customers better and maintain a competitive edge.

While certain DevOps principles, such as two-pizza teams and microservices/**service-oriented architecture** (**SOA**), fall beyond the scope of this discussion, this whitepaper focuses on Azure's CI/CD capability, a pivotal element in delivering software features swiftly and reliably.

Azure now provides these CI/CD capabilities through a suite of developer services: Azure DevOps Services, Azure Repos, Azure Pipelines, Azure Artifacts, and Azure Deploy. These services empower developers and IT operations professionals practicing DevOps to securely and rapidly deliver software. Together, they facilitate the secure storage and application of version control to an application's source code. Azure DevOps Services allows for the seamless orchestration of an end-to-end software release workflow using these services. For existing environments, Azure Pipelines offers flexibility, enabling the integration of each service independently with existing tools. These services, accessible through the Azure portal, Azure APIs, and Azure SDKs, stand as highly available, easily integrated tools, reinforcing the overall efficiency of the Azure ecosystem.

Practices of CI/CD

This section discusses the practices of continuous integration and continuous delivery. We will explain the difference between continuous delivery and continuous deployment.

Continuous integration

CI is a software development methodology wherein developers consistently integrate code modifications into a central repository, triggering automated builds and tests thereafter. CI predominantly addresses the build or integration phase of the software release process, necessitating both an automated element (like a CI or build service) and a cultural element (such as adopting frequent integration practices). The primary objectives of CI revolve around the prompt identification and resolution of bugs, enhancement of software quality, and reduction of the time taken to validate and release new software updates.

CI places emphasis on incorporating smaller code commits and incremental code changes. Developers commit code at regular intervals, with a minimum frequency of once a day. Before pushing to the build server, developers pull code from the repository to ensure local host code is merged. At this juncture, the build server executes various tests, and either approves or rejects the code commit.

The fundamental challenges in implementing CI encompass the introduction of more frequent commits to the shared codebase, maintenance of a singular source code repository, automation of builds, and automation of testing. Further challenges include conducting tests in environments resembling production, ensuring transparency of the process for the team, and facilitating developers in easily accessing any version of the application.

Continuous delivery and deployment

CD is a software development methodology wherein alterations to the code undergo automatic building, testing, and preparation for deployment to production. CI is extended by deploying code changes to the testing and production environment, in addition to completing the build stage. Continuous delivery can be entirely automated through a streamlined workflow or partially automated, incorporating manual steps at crucial junctures. When executed effectively, continuous delivery ensures that developers consistently possess a deployment-ready build artifact that has successfully traversed a standardized testing process.

In contrast, continuous deployment takes automation a step further by automatically deploying revisions to a production environment without requiring explicit approval from a developer. This fully automated approach streamlines the entire software release process, fostering a continuous feedback loop with customers early in the product lifecycle.

Distinguishing continuous delivery from continuous deployment

A common misconception regarding CD is that it implies the immediate application of every committed change to production after successfully passing automated tests. However, the essence of CD lies not in instantly applying every change to production, but in ensuring that each change is prepared for production.

Before deploying a change to production, you can establish a decision-making process, ensuring that the deployment to production is authorized and subject to audit. This decision can be made by an individual and subsequently executed by the tools in use.

With CD, the decision to go live transforms into a business decision rather than a technical one. The technical validation occurs with every commit.

Introducing a change to production does not constitute a disruptive event. The deployment process does not necessitate the technical team halting work on subsequent changes and does not require a project plan, handover documentation, or a dedicated maintenance window. Deployment evolves into a replicable process, having been executed and validated multiple times in testing environments.

Advantages of continuous delivery

CD offers various advantages to your software development team, encompassing the automation of processes, heightened developer productivity, elevated code quality, and the expedited delivery of updates to your customers.

Automating the release process

CD furnishes a mechanism for your team to commit code that undergoes automatic building, testing, and preparation for release to production. This ensures that your software delivery process is not only efficient and resilient but also rapid and secure.

Enhancing developer efficiency

Implementing CD practices enhance your team's productivity by liberating developers from manual tasks, unraveling intricate dependencies, and redirecting their attention to the core task of delivering novel features in software. Rather than grappling with the integration of their code across different business components and allocating time to figure out the deployment intricacies, developers can concentrate on crafting the logical code that brings forth the desired features.

Enhancing code quality

CD aids in the early detection and resolution of bugs in the delivery process, preventing them from evolving into more significant issues later on. The automation of the entire process facilitates the seamless execution of various types of code tests. Through a disciplined approach of conducting more tests at higher frequencies, teams can iterate rapidly, receiving immediate feedback on the consequences of changes. This empowers teams to produce high-quality code with a robust assurance of stability and security. Developers receive prompt feedback, allowing them to ascertain the functionality of new code and identify any introduced breaking changes or bugs. Addressing mistakes early in the development process is notably more straightforward.

Accelerate update delivery

CD empowers your team to rapidly and regularly deliver updates to customers. The implementation of CI/CD elevates the overall velocity of the team, expediting the release of both features and bug fixes. This heightened efficiency enables enterprises to respond promptly to market changes, security demands, evolving customer needs, and cost pressures. For instance, if there is a need for a new security feature, implementing CI/CD with automated testing allows your team to swiftly and reliably introduce the fix to production systems with a high level of confidence. Tasks that previously consumed weeks or months can now be accomplished in a matter of days or even hours.

Implementing CI/CD

In this section, we will delve into the steps you can take to initiate the adoption of a CI/CD model within your organization, specifically tailored for the Azure environment. It is important to clarify that our focus here does not cover the intricacies of how an organization with an advanced DevOps and cloud transformation model builds and employs an Azure-specific CI/CD pipeline. For additional resources and tools relevant to this topic, consider seeking guidance from experts and specialists in the Azure ecosystem. If you are looking for insights on preparing for a transition to the Azure Cloud, consult the Azure Cloud Transformation Maturity documentation for more comprehensive information.

Navigating the route to CI/CD

Visualizing CI/CD resembles a pipeline (refer to *Figure 7.1*), wherein fresh code is introduced at one end, undergoes testing across various stages (source, build, staging, and production), and ultimately emerges as production-ready code. For organizations new to CI/CD, it is advisable to approach this pipeline iteratively. This implies commencing with a modest scale and iterating at each stage, allowing for a gradual understanding and refinement of the code development process conducive to the growth of your organization. Please refer to the following figure:

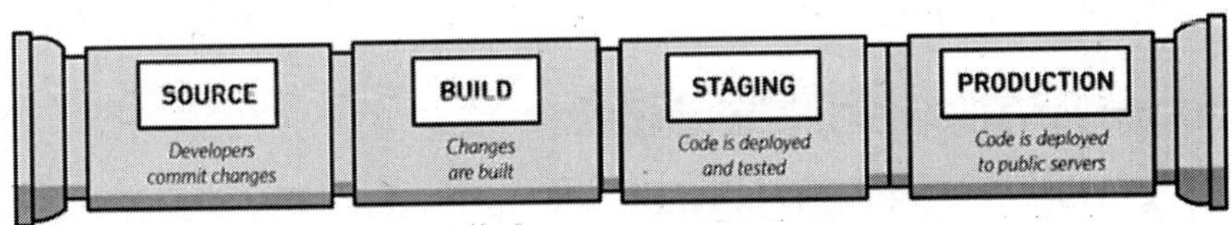

Figure 7.1: *CI/CD pipeline*

Each stage of the CI/CD pipeline serves as a distinct step in the delivery process, functioning as a checkpoint to evaluate specific aspects of the code. The underlying assumption is that, as the code advances through the pipeline, its quality improves because a more comprehensive verification process unfolds. Any issues identified in an early stage act as a barrier, preventing the code from advancing further in the pipeline. Immediate notifications are sent to the team upon test results, and all subsequent builds and releases are halted if the software fails to pass a particular stage.

While these stages are presented as suggestions, you have the flexibility to adapt them based on your business requirements. Some stages can be duplicated to accommodate various types of testing, including security and performance. Depending on your project's complexity and team structure, certain stages might need repetition at different levels. For instance, the output of one team can become a dependency in the subsequent team's project, signifying that the first team's final product serves as an artifact in the next team's project.

The implementation of a CI/CD pipeline significantly influences the maturation of your organization's capabilities. It is advisable to commence with incremental steps rather than attempting to establish a fully mature pipeline with multiple environments, numerous testing phases, and automation across all stages from the outset. It is crucial to acknowledge that even organizations with highly mature CI/CD environments continually refine and enhance their pipelines.

Transforming into a CI/CD-enabled organization is an ongoing journey with numerous milestones. In the subsequent section, we explore a potential pathway for your organization, commencing with continuous integration and progressing through the tiers of continuous delivery.

As an organization, building a CI/CD enabled environment is a journey with many destinations. In the following section, we will discuss a possible pathway your organization might take, starting from continuous integration and progressing through the stages of continuous delivery.

Continuous integration

CI/CD journey involves cultivating maturity in CI, where developers consistently commit code to a central repository, hosted on platforms like CodeCommit or GitHub. This commitment extends to merging all changes into a designated release branch for the application. The ethos of continuous integration discourages isolated code holding, emphasizing the importance of keeping feature branches updated through frequent merging. The team is encouraged to make frequent commits and merges, fostering discipline and aligning seamlessly with the overarching CI/CD process. Proactive creation of unit tests during early application development is complemented by running tests before pushing code to the central repository, serving as a strategy for identifying errors. Once code is pushed, a workflow engine monitors the branch and triggers a command to a builder tool, initiating code build and unit tests. This process, appropriately scaled for swift feedback, integrates quality checks like unit test coverage, style checks, and static analysis. The CI phase, emphasizing collaboration, disciplined coding practices, and proactive testing, establishes a solid foundation for subsequent CI/CD pipeline stages, accelerating development cycles and fortifying the reliability and quality of the evolving software. Refer to the following figure:

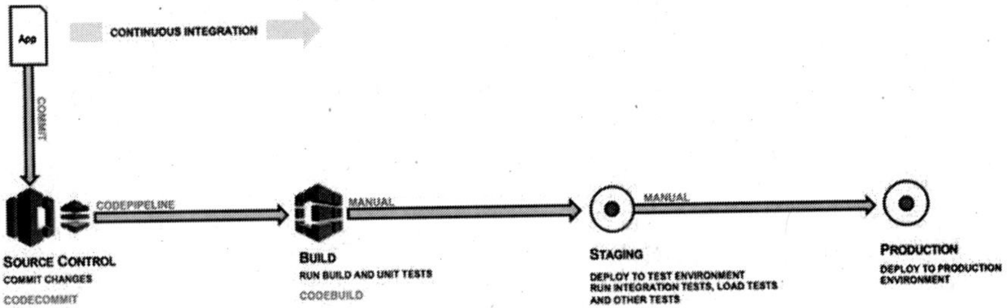

Figure 7.2: *CI: Source and build*

The initial phase in the CI/CD journey involves cultivating maturity in continuous integration. It is essential to ensure that developers consistently commit their code to a central repository, hosted, for instance, in CodeCommit or GitHub, and merge all changes into a designated release branch for the application. The practice discourages developers from holding code in isolation, emphasizing the importance of keeping feature branches up to date through frequent merging from upstream. The team is encouraged to make frequent commits and merges, incorporating complete units of work, fostering discipline and aligning with the overall process. A developer who merges code early and regularly is likely to encounter fewer integration issues in the future.

Furthermore, developers should create unit tests during early stages of application development and run them prior to pushing the code to the central repository. Identifying errors/bugs in the early stages of software development is both cost-effective and easier to address.

After pushing code to a branch in the source code repository, a workflow engine monitors the branch and triggers a command to a builder tool. This initiates the code build and unit tests in a controlled environment. The build process should be appropriately scaled to manage all activities, including pushes and tests during the commit stage, ensuring swift feedback. Additional quality checks, such as unit test coverage, style checks, and static analysis, can also be integrated at this stage. Ultimately, the builder tool generates one or more binary builds and other artifacts, such as images, stylesheets, and documents, for the application.

Continuous delivery: Creating a staging environment

Moving on to the CD phase, this involves deploying the application code in a staging environment, mirroring the production stack, and conducting additional functional tests. Refer to the following figure:

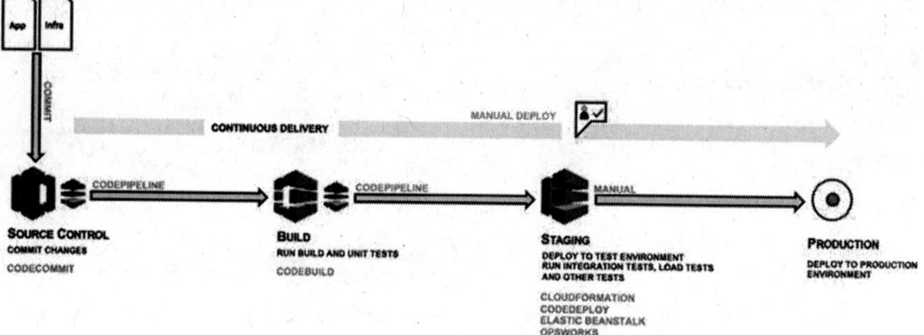

Figure 7.3: Continuous delivery: Staging

The staging environment can either be a pre-established static environment designed for testing purposes, or it can be a dynamically provisioned and configured environment with committed infrastructure and configuration code, tailored for testing and deploying the application code.

Continuous delivery: Creating a production environment

Moving on to the CD phase, the crucial aspect is creating a production environment that mirrors the staging environment where functional tests are conducted. Refer to the following figure:

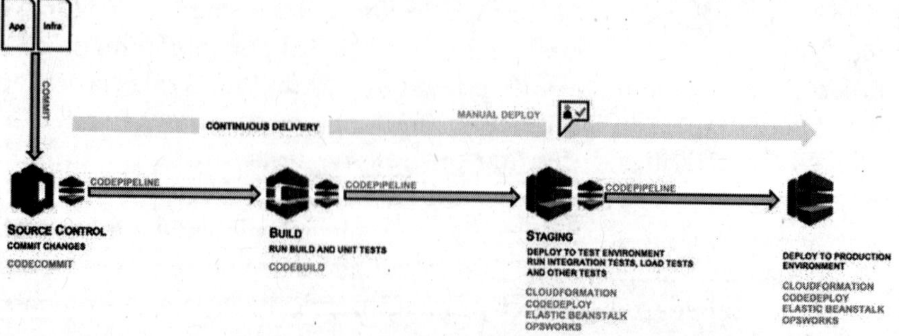

Figure 7.4: Continuous delivery: Production

Once the **Infrastructure as Code** (**IaC**) has been used to build the staging environment, creating a production environment in the same way becomes a quick and easy task.

Continuous deployment

This is the final step of the CI/CD pipeline. Continuous deployment involves automating the entire process of releasing software, including the deployment to the production environment. Refer to the following figure:

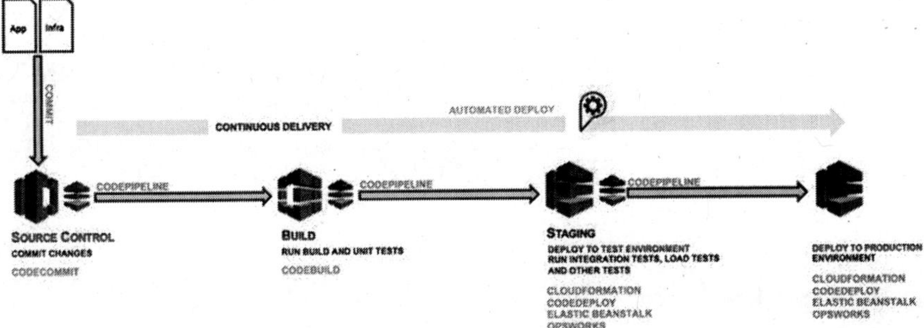

Figure 7.5: *Continuous deployment*

In a well-established CI/CD environment, the path to the production environment is completely automated, ensuring that the code can be deployed with a high level of confidence.

Maturity and beyond

As your organization grows, your CI/CD model will evolve to include more improvements such as the following:

- Adding more staging environments that cater to specific requirements like performance, compliance, security, and **user interface** (**UI**) tests.
- Conducting unit tests for not only application code but also infrastructure and configuration code.
- Integrating with other systems and processes like code review, issue tracking, and event notification.
- Integrating with database schema migration (where applicable).
- Adding more steps for auditing and business approval.

Even the most mature organizations with complex multi-environment CI/CD pipelines continue to seek improvements. DevOps is a continuous ongoing journey, not a destination. Feedback is continuously gathered about the pipeline, and improvements in speed, scale, security, and reliability are achieved through collaboration between different parts of the development teams.

Teams

Azure suggests structuring three developer teams for establishing a CI/CD environment: An application team, an infrastructure team, and a tools team (refer to *Figure 7.6*). This organizational model reflects a collection of best practices derived from the experiences of dynamic startups, large enterprise entities, and Amazon's own practices. This adheres to the communication rule, recognizing that meaningful conversations face limitations as group sizes expand and lines of communication increase.

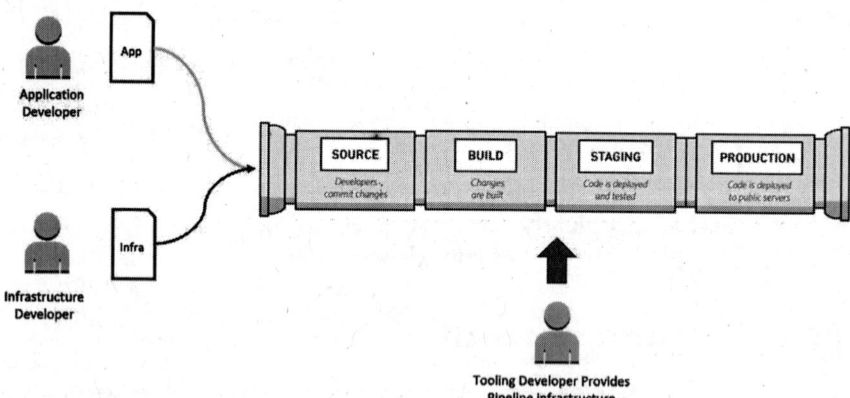

Figure 7.6: *Application, infrastructure, and tools teams*

Application team

The application team is responsible for developing the application. Application developers take ownership of the backlog, stories, and unit tests, working on features aligned with a defined application target. The team's overarching objective is to reduce the time spent by developers on non-core application tasks.

Beyond possessing functional programming skills in the application language, the application team should also have proficiency in platform skills and a comprehension of system configuration. This dual expertise allows them to concentrate on feature development and fortify the application without distractions.

Infrastructure team

The infrastructure team at Azure is responsible for crafting the code that creates and configures the infrastructure necessary to run the application. This team may utilize native Azure tools, such as **Azure Resource Manager** (**ARM**) templates, or general-purpose tools like Chef, Puppet, or Ansible. Collaborating closely with the application and infrastructure team specifies the required resources. For smaller applications, this team may consist of only one or two individuals.

Proficiency in infrastructure provisioning methods, such as ARM templates or Terraform, is crucial for the team. They should also develop configuration automation skills using tools like Chef, Ansible, Puppet, or Salt.

Tools team

The tools team builds and manages the CI/CD pipeline. They are responsible for the infrastructure and tools that make up the pipeline. They do not belong to the team with a size limited to what two large size pizzas can feed, however they create a tool that is used by the application and infrastructure teams in the organization. The organization needs to continuously mature its tools team, so that the tools team stays one step ahead of the maturing application and infrastructure teams.

The tools team must be skilled in building and integrating all parts of the CI/CD pipeline. This includes building source control repositories, workflow engines, build environments, testing frameworks, and artifact repositories. This team may choose to implement software such as AWS CodeStar, AWS CodePipeline, AWS CodeCommit, AWS CodeDeploy, and AWS CodeBuild, along with Jenkins, GitHub, Artifactory, TeamCenter, and other similar tools. Some organizations might call this a DevOps team, but we discourage this. Instead, we encourage thinking of DevOps as the sum of the people, processes, and tools in software delivery.

Testing stages in CI/CD

The three CI/CD teams should incorporate testing into the software development lifecycle at the different stages of the CI/CD pipeline.

Overall, testing should start as early as possible. The testing pyramid shown in the following figure is a concept provided by *Mike Cohn* in *Succeeding with Agile*. It shows the various software tests in relation to their cost and speed at which they run. Please refer to the following figure:

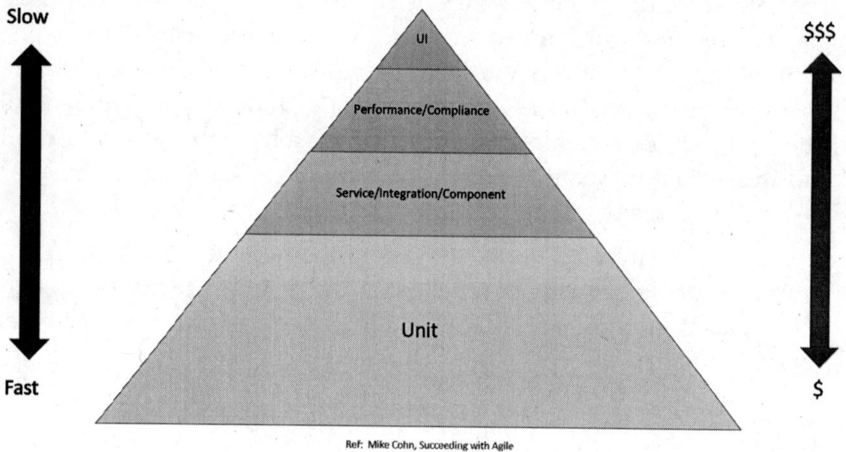

Figure 7.7: *CI/CD testing pyramid*

Unit tests should make around 70% of your testing strategy. They are the foundation of the pyramid, with quick execution and low cost. It is advisable to aim for near-complete code coverage in unit tests, as bugs identified at this stage can be rectified swiftly and inexpensively.

Moving up the pyramid are service, component, and integration tests, which necessitate intricate environments, rendering them more resource-intensive in terms of infrastructure and slower to execute. The subsequent level encompasses performance and compliance tests, which demand production-quality environments and incur higher costs. At the apex of the pyramid are UI and user acceptance tests, both requiring production-quality environments.

While all these tests contribute to a comprehensive strategy for ensuring high-quality software, the emphasis for expeditious development lies in the quantity of tests and coverage in the bottom half of the pyramid.

In the following sections, we will discuss the CI/CD stages.

Setting up the source

At the project's initiation, it is crucial to establish a repository to store your raw code, as well as configuration and schema changes. During the source stage, consider selecting a source code repository, such as one hosted on GitHub or Azure Repos.

Setting up and executing builds

Build automation is a vital aspect of the CI process. While setting up build automation, the first step is to choose the appropriate build tool. There are several build tools available for different programming languages, such as Ant, Maven, Gradle for Java, Make for C/C++, Grunt for JavaScript, and Rake for Ruby. The choice of the right build tool depends on the programming language of your project and the skills of your team.

Once the build tool is selected, all dependencies must be clearly defined in the build scripts along with the build steps. It is also a recommended practice to version the final build artifacts to make it easier to deploy and keep track of issues.

During the build stage, the build tools take any changes made to the source code repository as input, build the software, and run various tests, including:

- **Unit testing:** Unit testing is a process that checks a specific portion of the code to ensure that it performs as expected. This type of testing is carried out by software developers during the development phase. At this stage, software verification processes like static code analysis, data flow analysis and code coverage can be applied.
- **Static code analysis:** Static code analysis is a test performed without executing the application after the build and unit testing. This analysis is useful in finding coding errors, security holes, and ensuring that coding guidelines are followed.

Staging

During the staging phase, complete environments replicating the eventual production environment are created. The following tests are conducted:

- **Integration testing:** This verifies the interfaces between various components against the software design. Integration testing is an ongoing process that helps build robust interfaces and system integrity.

- **Component testing:** This test checks the message passing between various components and their outcomes. A key aim of this testing could be idempotency in component testing. Tests can include extremely large data volumes, edge cases, and abnormal inputs.
- **System testing:** This verifies the system end-to-end and confirms if the software fulfills the business requirement. This might involve testing the UI, API, back-end logic, and end state.
- **Performance testing:** Performance testing evaluates the responsiveness and stability of a system under a particular workload. It plays an essential role in software development, helping to ensure that the system meets the desired quality standards in terms of scalability, reliability, and resource usage. Different types of performance tests, including load tests, stress tests, and spike tests, are used to benchmark the system against predefined criteria.
- **Compliance testing:** Compliance testing checks whether the code change adheres to the requirements of a non-functional specification and/or regulations. It determines if the defined standards are being implemented and met.
- **UAT (User Acceptance Testing):** UAT validates the end-to-end business flow and is executed by an end-user in a staging environment. It confirms whether the system meets the requirements of the requirement specification. Alpha and beta testing methodologies are commonly used at this stage.
- **Production testing:** Production involves repeating the staging phase in a production environment after passing the previous tests. In this phase, the new code can be tested on a small subset of servers or even one Region before deploying it to the entire production environment.

Specifics on how to safely deploy to production are covered in the *Deployment methods* section.

Next, we will build the pipeline to incorporate these stages and tests.

Building the pipeline

In this segment, we will explore the construction of the pipeline. Begin by creating a pipeline with the essential components for CI and subsequently evolve it into a CD pipeline with additional components and stages. The discussion in this section also delves into the potential utilization of Azure Functions and manual approvals, especially pertinent for expansive projects. Additionally, considerations are outlined for planning across multiple teams, branches, and Azure regions.

Starting with a minimum viable pipeline for continuous integration

Your organization's journey toward CD begins with a **minimum viable pipeline** (**MVP**). As discussed in continuous delivery maturity, teams can start with a very simple process, such as implementing a pipeline that performs a code style check or a single unit test without deployment.

A vital element in this context is a continuous delivery orchestration tool. To facilitate the construction of this pipeline, Microsoft Azure provides tools such as Azure DevOps for seamless integration and automation. Refer to the following figure:

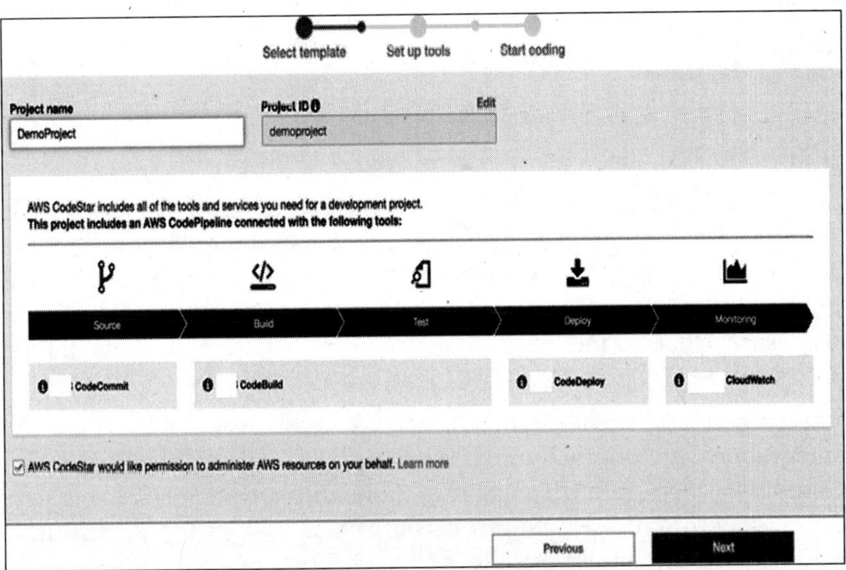

***Figure 7.8:** Azure setup page*

Azure DevOps utilizes a combination of Azure Pipelines, Azure Repos, Azure Artifacts, and Azure Boards, offering an integrated setup process, tools, templates, and a comprehensive dashboard. Azure

DevOps provides a complete solution for efficiently developing, building, and deploying applications on the Azure platform. This enables a faster release of code. Users already acquainted with the Azure portal and desiring a more hands-on approach can manually configure their preferred developer tools and provision individual Azure services as required. Refer to the following figure:

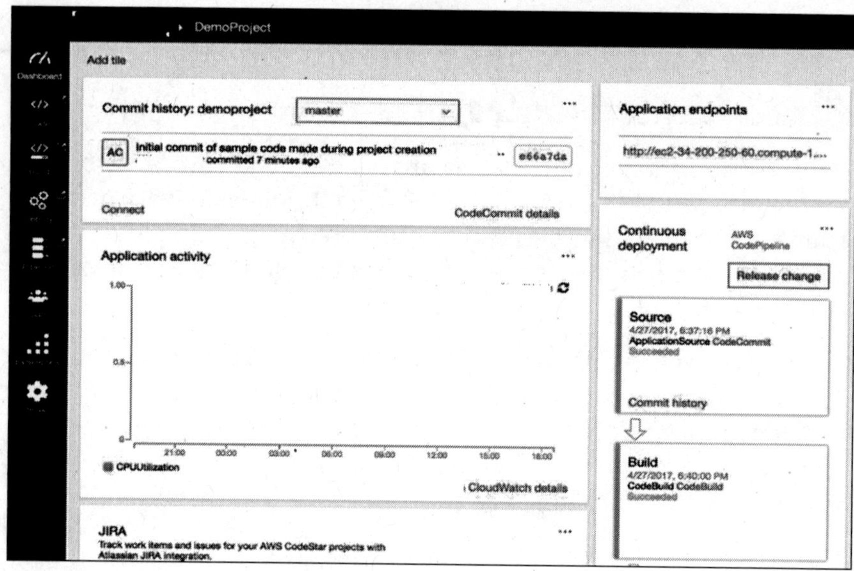

Figure 7.9: Azure dashboard

Azure DevOps provides Azure Pipelines, a CI/CD service that can be accessed either through the Azure DevOps platform or directly through the Azure portal for swift and dependable application and infrastructure updates. Azure Pipelines automate the build, testing, and deployment processes each time there is a code change, adhering to the release process models defined by users. This capability facilitates the rapid and reliable delivery of features and updates.

Creating a comprehensive solution is made easy with pre-built integrations for popular third-party services, such as GitHub, or by seamlessly incorporating custom plugins into any stage of the release process. With Azure Pipelines, you only incur charges for the resources you use, eliminating upfront fees or long-term commitments.

The stages of Azure DevOps and Azure Pipelines align directly with the source, build, staging, and production phases of CI/CD. While CD is the ultimate goal, you have the flexibility to initiate with a straightforward two-step pipeline that checks the source repository and executes a build action. Refer to the following figure:

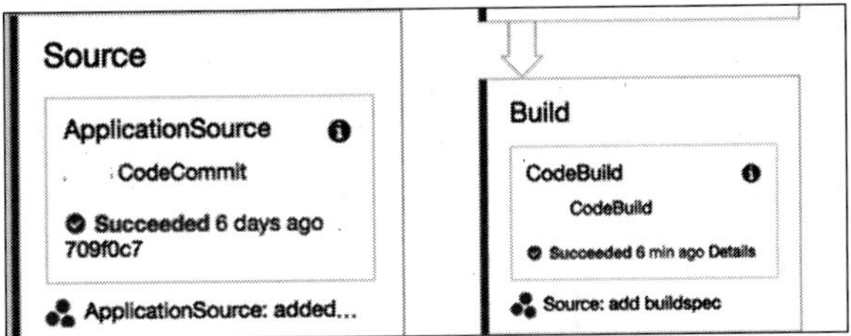

Figure 7.10: Azure code pipeline: Source and build stages

For Azure Pipelines, the source stage can intake inputs from various repositories, including GitHub, Azure Repos, and Azure Artifacts. Automating the build process marks a crucial initial phase in implementing continuous delivery and progressing toward continuous deployment. By eliminating manual intervention in the generation of build artifacts, you relieve your team of burdens, reduce the likelihood of errors introduced during manual packaging, and enable more frequent packaging of consumable artifacts.

Azure Pipelines seamlessly integrate with Azure DevOps Services, offering a fully managed build service known as **Azure Pipelines Build**. This allows you to effortlessly configure a build step within your pipeline to package your code and execute unit tests. With Azure Pipelines Build, there is no need to provision, manage, or scale your build servers, as it automatically scales and concurrently processes multiple builds to prevent queuing delays. Azure Pipelines also supports integration with popular build servers such as Jenkins and TeamCity.

For instance, in the build stage depicted in the following figure, three actions (unit testing, code style checks, and code metrics collection) run concurrently. Using Azure Pipelines Build, these steps can be incorporated as new tasks without the need for additional effort in building or installing build servers to handle the workload.

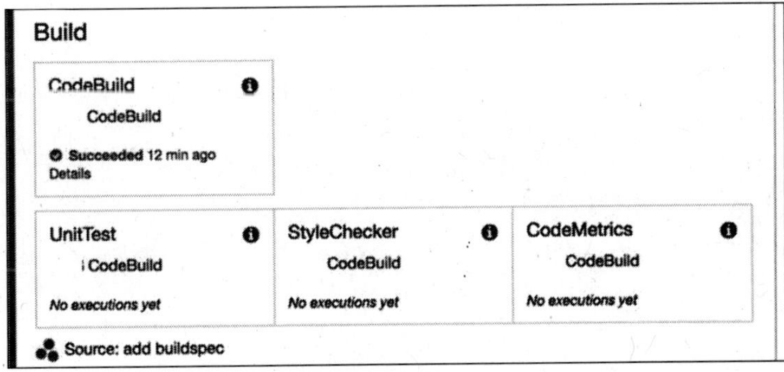

Figure 7.11: Azure code pipeline: Build functionality

The source and build stages illustrated in *Figure 7.10*, coupled with associated processes and automation, facilitate your team's progression toward CI. In this stage of maturity, developers must consistently monitor build and test outcomes while cultivating and sustaining a robust unit test suite. This practice contributes to enhancing the team's confidence in the CI/CD pipeline, promoting its widespread adoption.

Continuous delivery pipeline

Once the CI pipeline is in place, and supporting processes are established, your teams can initiate the shift toward a CD pipeline. This transition necessitates the automation of both building and deploying applications.

A CD pipeline distinguishes itself by introducing staging and production stages, with the production stage requiring manual approval.

In the same manner as the CI pipeline was built, your teams can gradually start building a CD pipeline by writing their deployment scripts.

Depending on the application's requirements, some deployment steps can be abstracted using existing Azure services. For instance, Azure DevOps directly integrates with Azure Deployment Manager, a service automating code deployments to Azure virtual machines and on-premises instances, Azure Automation, a configuration management service supporting operations with tools like PowerShell, and Azure App Service, a platform for deploying and expanding web applications and services.

Azure provides comprehensive documentation on implementing and integrating Azure Deployment Manager with your infrastructure and pipeline. Please refer to the *Microsoft Azure* documentation for more details.

Once the deployment of the application is successfully automated, deployment stages can be expanded to include various tests, enhancing the overall reliability of the process.

After your team successfully automates the deployment of the application, deployment stages can be expanded with various tests. An example is depicted in the following figure:

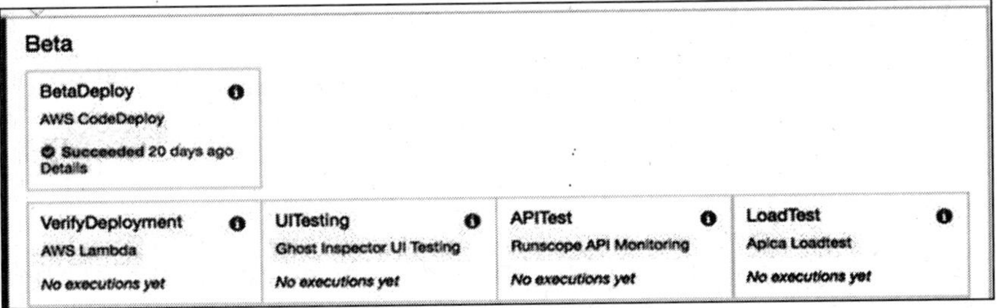

***Figure 7.12:** Azure code pipeline: Code tests in deployment stages*

You have the option to incorporate additional pre-built integrations with services such as Ghost Inspector, Runscope, Apica, and various others.

Adding actions

Azure DevOps and Azure Pipelines facilitate integration with Azure Functions. This integration empowers the execution of a wide array of tasks, including the creation of custom resources in your environment, seamless integration with third-party systems (such as Slack), and conducting checks on your recently deployed environment.

Functions can be used in CI/CD pipelines to do the following tasks:

- You can implement changes in your Azure environment by applying or updating an Azure Cloud template.
- Create Azure Cloud resources on demand in one pipeline stage and delete in another.
- Deploy application versions with zero downtime. Implement zero-downtime deployment of application versions on Azure App Service, leveraging an Azure Function to seamlessly swap CNAME values.
- Deploy to Docker instances on **Azure Container Instances (ACI)**.
- Before building or deploying, create a snapshot to back up resources.
- Additionally, integrate third-party products into your pipeline, such as posting messages to an RTC client.

Manual approvals

To add an approval action to a stage in a pipeline, you can choose the point where you want the pipeline execution to stop. This will allow someone with the necessary Azure Identity and identity access management permissions to approve or reject the action.

Once an action is approved, the pipeline execution will continue. However, if the action is rejected or if no one approves or rejects the action within seven days of the pipeline stopping at the action, it will be considered as a failed action and the pipeline execution will not continue. Refer to the following figure:

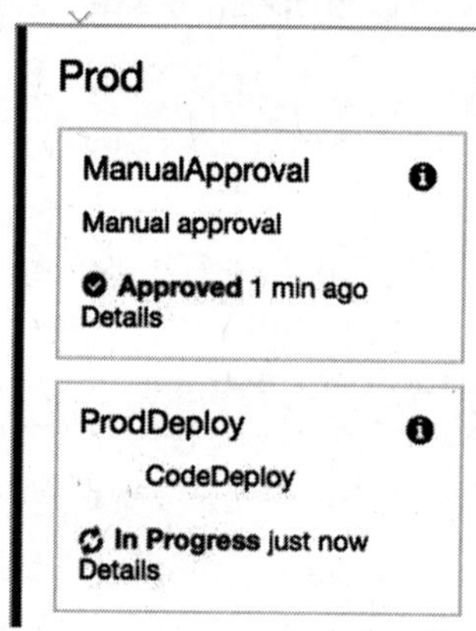

Figure 7.13: *Azure code deploy manual approvals*

Deploying infrastructure code changes in a CI/CD pipeline

Azure Pipelines allows you to incorporate ARM templates as a deployment action at any stage in your pipeline. Subsequently, you can specify the particular action you want ARM templates to execute, such as creating or deleting resource groups and initiating or executing change sets. A resource group in Azure corresponds to the concept of a stack in AWS CloudFormation and denotes a collection of interconnected Azure resources. While there are diverse approaches to provisioning IaC, Azure ARM templates serve as a robust, comprehensive tool endorsed by Azure, offering a scalable solution capable of describing an extensive range of Azure resources as code. For optimal results, we recommend utilizing Azure ARM templates within an Azure Pipelines project to monitor infrastructure modifications and conduct tests.

CI/CD for serverless applications

Azure DevOps, Azure Pipelines, Azure DevTest Labs, and ARM can be utilized to construct CI/CD pipelines tailored for serverless applications. These applications rely on Azure Functions, which are event-triggered, serverless compute resources. If you are a serverless application developer, you can leverage the integration of Azure Pipelines, Azure DevTest Labs, and ARM to streamline the automation of building, testing, and deploying serverless applications articulated through templates created with the ARM. **https://learn.microsoft.com/en-us/azure/architecture/serverless/guide/serverless-app-cicd-best-practices.**

Pipelines for multiple teams, branches, and regions

For a large project, it is not uncommon for multiple project teams to work on different components. If multiple teams use a single code repository, it can be mapped so that each team has its own branch. There should be an integration or release branch for the final merge of the project. If a service- oriented or microservice architecture is used, each team could have its own code repository.

In the first scenario, if a single pipeline is used, it is possible that one team could affect the other teams' progress by blocking the pipeline. We recommend that you create specific pipelines for the team branches and another release pipeline for the final product delivery.

Pipeline integration with Azure code build

Azure DevOps provides Azure Pipelines, designed to empower your organization in establishing a highly available build process with virtually limitless scalability. Azure Pipelines offer quickstart environments for various popular languages and the capability to execute any Docker container specified by your organization.

Benefiting from seamless integration with Azure Repos, Azure Pipelines, and Azure DevOps Services, along with support for Git and Azure Functions, the Azure Pipelines tool proves to be remarkably versatile.

Software can be compiled by incorporating a **`build.yaml`** file that delineates each of the build steps, encompassing pre- and post-build actions, or by defining actions directly through the Azure Pipelines tool.

To scrutinize the detailed history of each build, Azure Pipelines provides a comprehensive dashboard. All events are archived as log files in Azure Monitor. Refer to the following figure:

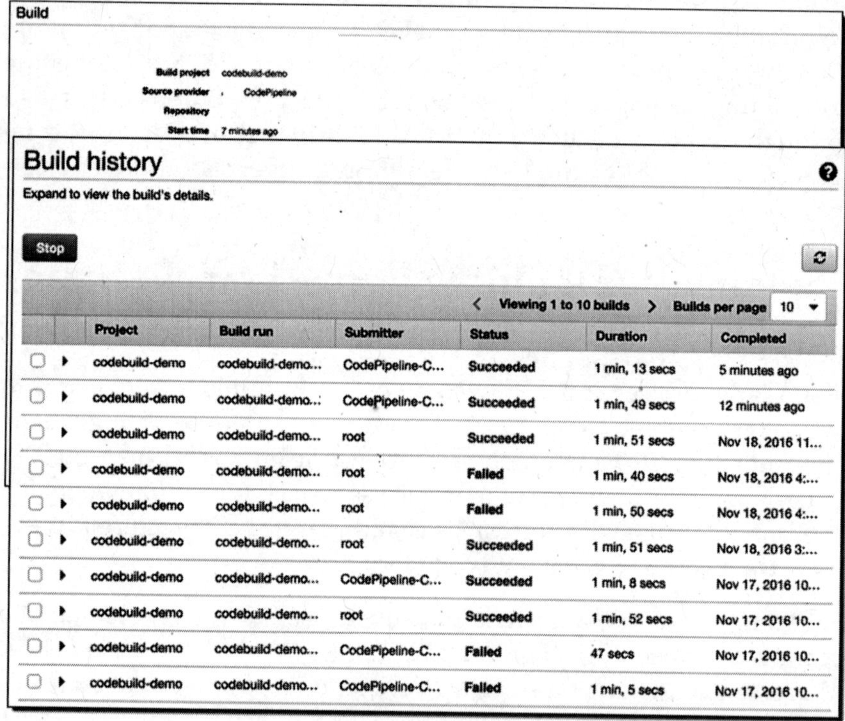

Project	Build run	Submitter	Status	Duration	Completed
codebuild-demo	codebuild-demo...	CodePipeline-C...	Succeeded	1 min, 13 secs	5 minutes ago
codebuild-demo	codebuild-demo...	CodePipeline-C...	Succeeded	1 min, 49 secs	12 minutes ago
codebuild-demo	codebuild-demo...	root	Succeeded	1 min, 51 secs	Nov 18, 2016 11...
codebuild-demo	codebuild-demo...	root	Failed	1 min, 40 secs	Nov 18, 2016 4:...
codebuild-demo	codebuild-demo...	root	Failed	1 min, 50 secs	Nov 18, 2016 4:...
codebuild-demo	codebuild-demo...	root	Succeeded	1 min, 51 secs	Nov 18, 2016 3:...
codebuild-demo	codebuild-demo...	CodePipeline-C...	Succeeded	1 min, 8 secs	Nov 17, 2016 10...
codebuild-demo	codebuild-demo...	root	Succeeded	1 min, 52 secs	Nov 17, 2016 10...
codebuild-demo	codebuild-demo...	CodePipeline-C...	Failed	47 secs	Nov 17, 2016 10...
codebuild-demo	codebuild-demo...	CodePipeline-C...	Failed	1 min, 5 secs	Nov 17, 2016 10...

Figure 7.14: *Logs log files in Azure code build*

Pipeline integration with Jenkins

Leveraging the Jenkins build tool allows you to construct delivery pipelines. These pipelines are constructed using conventional jobs that articulate the steps involved in executing continuous delivery stages. However, for larger projects, this approach may not be ideal due to the pipeline's current state not persisting between Jenkins restarts, challenges in straightforward implementation of manual approval, and complexities associated with tracking the state of an intricate pipeline.

We recommend implementation of CD with Jenkins using the Azure DevOps Pipeline plugin. The Pipeline plugin allows you to describe complex workflows using a Groovy-like domain-specific language and serves as a powerful tool to orchestrate intricate pipelines. Enhance the functionality of the Pipeline plugin by incorporating auxiliary plugins such as the Pipeline Stage View Plugin, which visualizes the current progress of stages defined in a pipeline, or the Pipeline Multibranch Plugin, allowing the grouping of builds from different branches.

We recommend that you store your pipeline configuration in *Jenkinsfile* and have it checked into a source code repository. This allows for tracking changes to pipeline code and becomes even more important when working with the Pipeline Multibranch Plugin. We also recommend that you divide your pipeline into stages. This logically groups the pipeline steps and also enables the Pipeline Stage View Plugin to visualize the current state of the pipeline.

Figure 7.15 shows a sample Jenkins pipeline, with four defined stages visualized by the Pipeline Stage View Plugin:

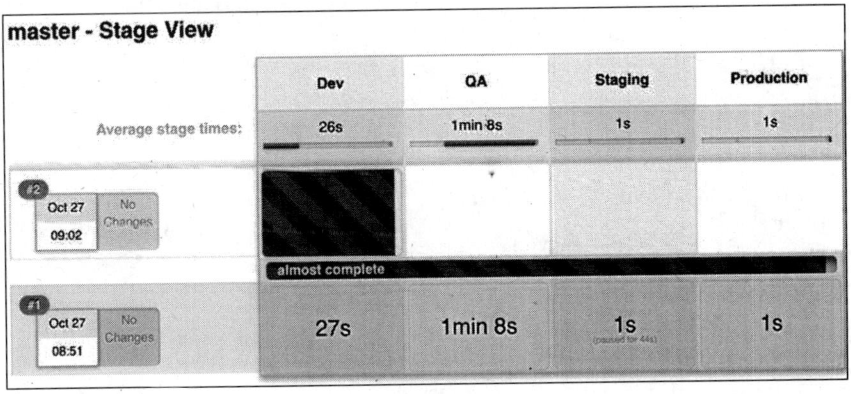

***Figure 7.15:** Defined stages of Jenkins pipeline visualized by the Pipeline Stage View Plugin*

Deployment methods

In a CD process, various deployment strategies and variations for introducing new software versions can be contemplated. This section delves into the prevalent deployment methods, including all at once (deploy in place), rolling, immutable, and blue/green. We specify the deployment methods supported by Azure DevOps and Azure App Service.

The following table summarizes the characteristics of each deployment method:

Method	Impact of failed deployment	Deploy time	Zero down-time	No DNS change	Rollback process	Code deployed to
Deploy in place	Downtime	🕒	X	✓	Re-deploy	Existing instances
Rolling	Single batch out of service. Any successful batches prior to failure running new application version.	🕒🕒 †	✓	✓	Re-deploy	Existing instances
Rolling with additional batch (beanstalk)	Minimal if first batch fails, otherwise similar to rolling.	🕒🕒🕒 †	✓	✓	Re-deploy	New & existing instances
Immutable	Minimal	🕒🕒🕒 🕒	✓	✓	Re-deploy	New instances
Blue/green	Minimal	🕒🕒🕒 🕒	✓	X	switch back to old environment	New instances

Table 7.1: *Comparison of deployment methods: Evaluating the impact, downtime, and rollback processes*

All at once: In-place deployment

Deploying all at once or in-place is a strategy for introducing new application code to an existing server fleet. This method involves replacing all the code in a single deployment action, leading to downtime as all servers in the fleet are simultaneously updated. Updating existing DNS records is unnecessary. In the event of a failed deployment, restoring operations involves redeploying the code on all servers once again.

In Azure App Service, this deployment approach is termed **All at Once**, and is applicable to single and load-balanced applications. In Azure DevOps, this deployment method is referred to as **in-place deployment**, with a deployment configuration labeled All at Once.

Rolling deployment

Through a rolling deployment, the server fleet is segmented, ensuring that the entire fleet is not upgraded simultaneously. This deployment process involves running two software versions, new and old, concurrently on the same fleet, allowing for a zero-downtime update. In case of deployment failure, only the updated portion of the fleet is affected.

A variant of the rolling deployment, known as a **canary release**, entails deploying the new software version on a very small percentage of servers initially. This approach enables the observation of how the software performs in a production environment on a limited number of servers, minimizing the impact of potential breaking changes. If a canary deployment results in an elevated error rate, the software is rolled back. Otherwise, the percentage of servers with the new version is gradually increased.

Azure App Service adopts the rolling deployment pattern with two deployment options, namely rolling and rolling with an additional batch. These options enable the application to initially scale up before removing servers from service, preserving full capability throughout the deployment. In Azure DevOps, this pattern is achieved as a variation of an in-place deployment, incorporating patterns such as OneAtATime and HalfAtATime.

Immutable and blue green deployment

The immutable pattern dictates deploying application code by initiating an entirely new set of servers with a fresh configuration or version of application code. This pattern capitalizes on the cloud's ability to create new server resources through straightforward API calls.

The blue-green deployment strategy falls under the category of immutable deployment, necessitating the creation of an additional environment. After the new environment is operational and successfully passes all tests, traffic is redirected to this new deployment. The old environment is referred to as the **blue** environment and is maintained in an idle state in case a rollback is required.

Azure App Service facilitates both immutable and blue green deployment patterns. In Azure DevOps, the blue green pattern is also supported.

Modification to database schema

It is commonplace for modern software to incorporate a database layer, typically utilizing a relational database that stores both data and its structure. Modifications to the database are often necessary within the continuous delivery process.

Addressing changes in a relational database poses distinct challenges compared to deploying application binaries. Unlike upgrading an application binary, where you can stop, upgrade, and restart the application without much concern for the application state, upgrading databases requires careful consideration of state preservation, given that a database contains substantial state alongside relatively less logic and structure.

Viewing the database schema before and after a change as different versions, tools like Liquibase and Flyway can be employed to manage these versions. Generally, these tools follow methods such as.

These tools utilize variations of the following approaches:

- Introducing a table to the database to store the database version.
- Tracking database change commands and grouping them into versioned change sets. In Liquibase, these changes are stored in XML files, while Flyway handles change sets as separate SQL files or occasionally as distinct Java classes for more intricate transitions.
- When upgrading a database, Liquibase examines the metadata table to determine which change sets to execute, bringing the database up to date with the latest version.

Outline of best practices

Here is a best practice with guidelines for CI/CD:

- **Do**
  - o Treat your infrastructure as code
    - ▪ Use version control for your infrastructure code.
    - ▪ Make use of bug tracking/ticketing systems.
    - ▪ Have peers review changes before applying them.

    - Establish infrastructure code patterns/designs.
    - Test infrastructure changes like code changes.
  - Put developers into integrated teams of no more than 12 self-sustaining members.
  - Have all developers commit code to the main trunk frequently, with no long-running feature branches.
  - Consistently adopt a build system such as Maven or Gradle across your organization and standardize builds.
  - Have developers build unit tests toward 100% coverage of the code base.
  - Ensure that unit tests are 70% of the overall testing in duration, number, and scope.
  - Ensure that unit tests are up-to-date and not neglected. Unit test failures should be fixed, not bypassed.
  - Treat your continuous delivery configuration as code.
  - Establish role-based security controls (that is, who can do what and when).
    - Monitor/track every resource possible.
    - Alert on services, availability, and response times.
    - Capture, learn, and improve.
    - Share access with everyone on the team.
    - Plan metrics and monitoring into the lifecycle.
  - Keep and track standard metrics.
    - Number of builds.
    - Number of deployments.
    - Average time for changes to reach production.
    - Average time from first pipeline stage to each stage.
    - Number of changes reaching production.
    - Average build time.
  - Use multiple distinct pipelines for each branch and team.
- **Do not**
  - Have long-running branches with large complicated merges.
  - Have manual tests.

- o Have manual approval processes, gates, code reviews, and security reviews.

Conclusion

CI/CD creates an optimal environment for your organization's application teams. Developers seamlessly submit code to a repository, initiating a process that involves integration, testing, deployment, subsequent testing, merging with infrastructure, undergoing security and quality reviews, and ultimately becoming deployable with a high level of assurance. This systematic approach, encompassing security and quality reviews, ensures deployable software with confidence.

The adoption of CI/CD leads to enhanced code quality, facilitating the swift and confident delivery of software updates and minimizing the risk of disruptive changes. The outcomes of each release can be cross-referenced with data from production and operations, serving as valuable insights for planning subsequent development cycles. This integration of CI/CD practices is a crucial aspect of your organization's journey towards effective DevOps and cloud transformation.

In the next chapter, we will discuss the role of culture in CI/CD and data CI/CD. The chapter explores the evolving data-centric practices, the impact of culture, and anticipates future trends. It aims to elucidate the relationship between culture and CI/CD, navigate cultural roles, explore future trends, and foster an understanding of data CI/CD.

CHAPTER 8
Data CI/CD: Emerging Trends and Roles

Introduction

In this chapter, we will explore the world of **continuous integration and continuous delivery** (**CI/CD**) and data CI/CD. We will discuss culture's role in shaping these processes and look at how it influences both CI/CD and data CI/CD. We will also examine data-centric practices and their cultural impacts.

We will also look into the future of CI/CD and data CI/CD. Staying ahead and understanding the trends shaping these domains can give us a competitive edge. To work better with software and data, we should do it right, do it fast, and make sure the data is accurate. If we keep doing this, we can create a great system for using data to build things in the future.

Structure

The chapter covers the following topics:

- Role of culture in CI/CD and data CI/CD
- Future of CI/CD and data CI/CD

Objectives

This chapter aims to explain how culture and CI/CD are related so the readers can gain a better understanding of this relationship. This includes understanding how culture influences CI/CD, cultural roles, gaining insights into future trends, adapting culture to align with CI/CD principles, and developing a holistic perspective on data CI/CD. By accomplishing these objectives, readers can gain insights into the changing technological landscape and create an environment that encourages innovation and efficiency.

Role of culture in CI/CD and data CI/CD

Culture plays a significant role in the world of CI/CD. It is the driving force that shapes the way these processes are carried out. To truly understand the significance of culture, we need to take a closer look at how it impacts the way we tackle the challenges of modern software development.

Collaboration and quality

The cornerstone of CI/CD and data CI/CD success lies in cultivating a culture that embodies collaboration and quality. This culture goes beyond adopting tools and processes; it signifies a fundamental shift in how an organization operates, collaborates, and perceives quality.

Collaboration

The following factors contribute to collaboration in software development:

- **Cross-functional teams:** Organizational structures must be reimagined to facilitate cross-functional teams. These teams comprise developers, testers, operations experts, and data specialists. They break down silos and instill a sense of shared ownership across the entire software development and deployment spectrum.
- **Effective communication ecosystem:** Open, transparent, and real-time communication channels are essential. Regular team

meetings, instant messaging platforms, and precise project status reporting create an environment of trust and shared responsibility.

- **Inclusive decision-making:** Embracing inclusive decision-making empowers individuals at all levels to contribute their insights and ideas. This inclusivity often leads to innovative solutions and a profound sense of ownership over the CI/CD and data CI/CD processes.
- **Conflict resolution mechanism:** A clear and established conflict resolution mechanism within cross-functional teams is essential. This mechanism covers processes, practices for addressing disagreements or other issues during the collaborative efforts. Often, this type of mechanism consists of open communication, structured approaches, and so on, to foster a healthy team dynamic.

Quality

Software quality necessitates an exhaustive and automated testing strategy. This strategy includes unit tests, integration tests, and end-to-end tests, acting as vigilant gatekeepers to detect and rectify issues in the nascent stages of development.

Establishing continuous monitoring mechanisms is crucial to ensuring the reliability of software in production. It involves tracking **Key Performance Indicators (KPIs)** and the proactive identification and resolution of anomalies.

A culture of quality thrives on feedback. Regular retrospectives and post-mortems serve as platforms for teams to analyze incidents and iterate continuously, leading to process enhancement and an elevated quality standard.

Data-driven decision-making culture

To achieve success in data CI/CD, it is important to cultivate a culture where data-driven decision-making is not just a goal, but a deeply embedded practice. It extends beyond data collection and storage to systematically harnessing data for informed choices and continuously enhancing products and processes.

Data-driven decision-making strategies for large projects

Some of the strategies related to large projects are:

- **Robust data governance framework:** A comprehensive framework is important to maintaining data quality, privacy, and security. It encompasses clearly defined data ownership, stringent access controls, and meticulous auditing mechanisms.
- **Investment in data literacy initiatives:** Organizations should invest in initiatives to enhance data literacy throughout the workforce. This includes comprehensive training programs, structured certification pathways, and resources fostering an understanding of data.
- **Data integration philosophy:** The shift toward a data-first mindset necessitates seamlessly integrating data practices into CI/CD workflows. Data pipelines are designed to parallel with application code, ensuring that data is readily accessible for analysis and decision-making.
- **Comprehensive testing:** A comprehensive testing framework that include not only the usual software testing but also has data quality and integrity components is essential for data-driven decision making. A thorough testing of data pipelines, ensure accurate data transformation, validation, and reliability must be ensured which contributes to the overall quality assurance of data-driven decision making.

CI/CD adoption

Leadership plays a crucial role in guiding an organization through the process of adopting transformative practices like CI/CD and data CI/CD. Effective leaders are not just observers but active promoters of these practices. They inspire their teams to follow their lead by setting an example and creating a shared vision that motivates everyone to embrace CI/CD and data CI/CD principles with enthusiasm and dedication.

Leadership strategies

The following strategies will showcase the essence of leadership by example, while adopting CI/CD practices:

- **Establishing a vision:** Leaders articulate a compelling vision for CI/CD and data CI/CD adoption, aligning it with the strategic objectives of the organization. Clear expectations, well-defined performance metrics, and measurable vital results (KPIs) are established to assess progress accurately.
- **Investment in knowledge and skill development:** Forward-thinking leaders invest substantially in the education and skill development of their teams. To effectively promote and encourage the adoption of CI/CD and data CI/CD practices, it is important to provide team members with easy access to the necessary resources and training materials. This could involve organizing workshops and training sessions to assist employees develop new skills and knowledge. Additionally, mentorship programs can play a valuable role in nurturing talent and supporting team members as they work to incorporate these practices into their work. By investing in these initiatives, organizations can help ensure that their workforce is well-equipped to succeed in an ever-evolving technological landscape.
- **Cultivating an ecosystem of innovation:** Leaders foster an environment where innovation thrives. They necessary resources and constant support for experimentation, cultivating a culture where employees feel comfortable experimenting with new ideas and learning from their mistakes. This helps to instill a *fail-fast, learn-fast* mindset within the team.

Future of CI/CD and data CI/CD

This section explores the changing landscape of CI/CD and data CI/CD. It discusses several trends, such as the evolution of GitOps, the integration of **Machine Learning** (**ML**), the importance of immutable infrastructure, and advancements in DataOps. It is predicted that there will be an era of AI-driven CI/CD and increased demand for data governance solutions. It also highlights the importance of edge computing. This section highlights the need for organizations to invest in people, processes, and technologies to deliver better results in the future and to encourage organizations to embrace innovation, collaboration, and a commitment to quality, speed, and data integrity to shape the future of CI/CD and data CI/CD.

Emerging trends

Closely tracking the latest trends shaping the future of CI/CD and data CI/CD practices, these developments have the potential to usher in significant shifts in software and data development approaches.

Evolution of GitOps

GitOps principles, which use Git repositories as the singular source of truth for infrastructure and application deployment, will undergo a transformative evolution. Innovative tools and practices will simplify the management of complex declarative configurations and catalyze the universal adoption of **Infrastructure as Code** (**IaC**).

Integrating ML into CI/CD pipelines seamlessly blends **Artificial Intelligence** (**AI**) and automation with software development. This integration will facilitate the automation of complex tasks, including model training, testing, and deployment, democratizing access to AI and ML capabilities across organizations.

Widespread adoption of immutable infrastructure

Immutable infrastructure patterns will emerge as the de facto standard, offering predictability in deployments and simplification in rollback procedures. Technologies such as containers and serverless computing will play a pivotal role in creating reliable and reproducible environments.

Advancements in DataOps

DataOps practices will undergo a metamorphosis to streamline data pipeline development and management. The automation of data pipeline testing, meticulous data lineage tracking, and seamless collaboration between data engineers and data scientists will become integral components of these practices.

Future predictions

Looking ahead, we will take a closer look at the latest trends shaping the future of CI/CD and data CI/CD practices. These trends could significantly change how we develop software and data.

One of the most exciting trends we expect to see is the rise of AI/ML in optimizing CI/CD pipelines. Predictive analytics and automation will become more sophisticated, allowing teams to identify and fix potential issues before they occur.

Another trend emerging is the increasing demand for advanced data governance solutions. With changing data regulations and a greater focus on data ethics, there will be a surge in comprehensive data cataloging, meticulous data lineage tracking, and granular access control mechanisms.

Finally, with edge computing expanding, we anticipate CI/CD pipelines will become more efficient in deploying applications and updates to edge devices. Specialized tools and practices for edge deployment will emerge as essential CI/CD ecosystem components.

Conclusion

As we wrap up, it is evident that the future of software and data development is intertwined with data. The convergence of CI/CD and data CI/CD methodologies is soon to be a reality, allowing for a smooth integration of data and applications. Ubiquity of immutable infrastructure. The organizations that focus on building a culture of collaboration, embracing data-driven approaches, and continuously improving their processes are poised to be at the forefront of the constantly evolving business landscape.

Companies need to invest in their people, processes, and technologies to thrive in this future that revolves around data. They must be adaptable and open to innovation, always ready to learn and embrace new things. To successfully improve the way we develop software and handle data, we need to focus on doing things well, doing them quickly, and making sure the data we work with is correct. If we stay committed to this approach, we can create a great system that will shape the future of how we use data to build things.

The future of CI/CD and data CI/CD is in your hands and holds limitless potential. Embrace it, and together, let us shape a future where data takes precedence, quality sets the standard, and innovation knows no bounds.

Join our book's Discord space

Join the book's Discord Workspace for Latest updates, Offers, Tech happenings around the world, New Release and Sessions with the Authors:

https://discord.bpbonline.com

Index

A

B

C

D

Q

R

S

T

U

V

W

X